Weaving without a loom

Weaving
without a loom

Barbara Pegg

A & C Black · London

First published 1986 by A & C Black (Publishers) Ltd
35 Bedford Row, London WC1R 4JH

Cover photograph by Jim Foreman of a tapestry
woven by the author

British Library Cataloguing in Publication Data

Pegg, Barbara
   Weaving without a loom.
   1. Hand weaving
   I. Title
   746.42   TT848

   ISBN 0-7136-2767-0

ISBN 0-7136-2767-0

Filmset in 10/12pt Photina by August Filmsetting,
Haydock.
Printed in Great Britain by
Hazell Watson & Viney Ltd, Aylesbury, Bucks

Contents

Colour plates after 16, 32, 64, 80, 96 and 104

Introduction

This book emphasises how much you can weave without necessarily having expensive or elaborate equipment. It is a culmination of ideas which have developed from my practising and teaching braid and tapestry weaving for a number of years, and I hope it will encourage and inspire you if you want to take up weaving, and, if you already are a weaver, will open up further possibilities. Essentially, *Weaving without a loom* is about how you can produce beautiful textiles with the use of a few simple tools.

Since I have been weaving, and looking at and reading about woven textiles, I have come to appreciate that for thousands of years weavers from many cultures throughout the world have woven exquisite and often very intricate textiles using the most apparently primitive equipment. That is not to say that the tools are by any means inadequate or amateur—a few sticks of wood holding a warp can be used in a great variety of ways: hung from upright poles like the Navajo Indians have done to make their blankets, or stretched along the ground as the Bedouin Arabs traditionally do to weave their rugs and tent coverings, or attached from the waist to a tree trunk as Guatemalan women do when weaving braids and huipils. The means by which these and other weavers have carried out their craft are carefully thought out, sturdy pieces of equipment which are portable, adaptable and readily available. Traditionally, the peasant weaver earned his or her living from the craft of weaving and in some parts of the world still does, so the weavers have tended to use what nature provides: sticks or bamboo for the loom, fibres spun from goat hair, or wool from sheep, or locally grown cotton coloured with natural dyes from plants to make cloth for their own needs or to take to market to sell. These days, the yarns may well be purchased from a local supplier, ready spun and dyed, but the tools on which the weaving is carried out remain more or less the same.

In recent years much more interest has been taken in the methods by which some of these strikingly beautiful textiles from all over the world have been woven, and this can, I think, inspire us to start weaving ourselves using some of these early methods. The bonus is that with such simple, inexpensive and portable tools we can begin to weave wherever and whenever we want, without the need for special workspace or equipment.

This book, then, is based on the grass roots of weaving. It concentrates on braid and tapestry weaving, both practised since weaving began two to three thousand years ago, but which can readily be adapted to contemporary ideas on colour and design, and can be used to make both functional and decorative pieces of weaving. The two main sections of the book on braids and tapestry are preceded by an introductory chapter which I have called 'About weaving', and which I think you will find valuable to read before you start to weave. It gives an overall view of what is involved in the type of weaving covered by the book. Details of basic equipment, weaving techniques and some projects are then described fully in each of the braid and tapestry sections. The final chapter on design is one which I felt it was important to include. The techniques of weaving are like a framework upon which you can hang your ideas. A successful piece of weaving is a fusion of technical skill and imaginative expression. Neither an exciting idea badly executed, nor a perfectly skilled piece of weaving which has no imagination will give you, the weaver, any real satisfaction, nor will it excite the viewer. Once you have mastered the techniques, you come to a stage where the expression of an idea, the use of colour and the execution of a design come into play and your weaving can take on a quality which is uniquely your own. I have tried, in 'Designing for weaving', to outline some of the major considerations when designing, and have suggested a few simple exercises which may serve as a springboard for ideas.

Weaving is a craft which has been practised for several thousand years and the woven textiles produced in the past reflected widely diverse cultures. Today, where many things are produced mechanically, we still have a desire to make things by hand because this allows us to assert our individuality and gives us enormous creative satisfaction. If you are a beginner to weaving, I hope these pages will inspire you to get started without the need for a lot of space and equipment; if you are an experienced loom weaver I hope that you find working in an alternative way using simple tools and traditional techniques will add a new perspective to your weaving.

About weaving

Definition of weaving

Weaving is a process in which pliable threads are interlaced with one another to form a fabric. The unique feature of a woven fabric, as opposed to a knitted, crocheted or lace fabric, is that it consists of two separate elements known as the warp and the weft. The warp is the set of threads which run along the length of the fabric and the weft is made up of separate threads which are passed through the warp widthways. The relationship between the warp and the weft can vary considerably as there are many different types of weave structure. I have outlined here the main structures which occur in this book. (Diag. 1, a to f).

Plain weave

Diagram 1

This is the simplest weave and produces a flat woven surface. In plain weave the weft passes over and under alternate warp ends (the term used for individual warp threads) in one row, then over and under the opposite warp ends in the next row. These two rows make up the entire structure and are repeated continuously. Plain weave can, however, take three different forms:

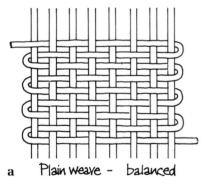

a Plain weave – balanced

Balanced weave
This weave, often called tabby, has an even balance between warp and weft with both showing equally. Some finger woven and backstrap braids have this weave structure.

Warp-faced weave
In this weave the warp ends are spaced very close together and the weft is pulled firmly across so the warp closes up completely. This results in a structure in which only the warp shows on the surface of the weave and the weft is invisible. In order to keep the edges neat, the weft is usually the same colour as the warp threads at the edges. Sometimes the weft is much thicker than the warp, giving a ribbed effect known as 'repp'. This effect is found in Peruvian finger braids. Warp-faced braids are common to backstrap and tablet weaving and are very strong.

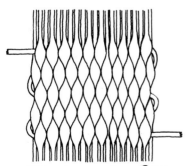

b Plain weave – warp-faced

Weft-faced weave

This weave is the reverse of warp-faced weave, because only the weft is visible and it completely covers the warp. In order to achieve this, the warp has to be a very strong, smooth cotton or linen, spaced far enough apart to allow the weft to be beaten down firmly. The weft is laid into the shed (the V shaped openings in the warp formed by raising alternate warp ends) loosely so that it can be pushed down with ease. Weft-faced weaves can occur in backstrap woven braids, and it is the weave structure which is always used in tapestry.

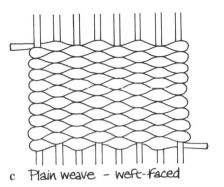

c Plain weave – weft-faced

Knots and loops

Knotting or looping the weft produces a weave structure with a textured surface.

Knots are cut threads introduced into the warp to give a pile and a more luxurious feel to the surface. The two commonest knots are called Ghiordes and Sennah. A row of knots is always interspaced by two rows of plain weave, usually beaten down as weft-faced weave so the knots are held firmly in place.

Knots can also be made with a continuous thread, and if they are left uncut they appear as loops on the surface of the weave. Pulling up weft threads and twisting them also makes looped pile.

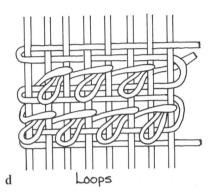

d Loops

Soumak

Soumak also has a textured surface, but is flatter and does not have a pile. It is a technique of looping a weft thread over and around warp ends in a sequence, to give a thick textured surface to the weave. Like knots, it is combined with plain weave for strength.

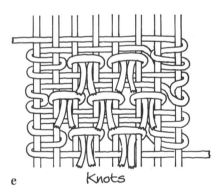

e Knots

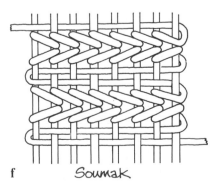

f Soumak

Weaving without a loom

Trying to create the weave structures just described would be possible, but tedious, if we tried to interlace the threads together by hand. To pass the weft through the warp more easily, the warp needs to be held in tension. It is for this reason that some device, whether primitive or sophisticated, is used to hold the warp. This device, then, is a warp-stretcher and the most elaborate type of these has come to be called a loom, but there are very many less complicated ways of stretching the warp. This book concentrates on what you can weave using the simplest kinds of warp-stretchers. Each section in the book shows you how much you can do with a few simple tools. Finger weaving requires a board and pins, backstrap weaving uses wooden sticks and a belt, tablet weaving needs small square cards and a belt, and tapestry is carried out on a simple frame.

The weaving process

First of all let's go through the different stages in weaving. The weaving process consists of:

1 Selecting yarns
2 Preparing the warp
3 Tensioning and spacing the warp
4 Making sheds in the warp
5 Preparing the weft
6 Weaving the weft through the warp
7 Removing the weaving and finishing off

Selecting yarns

Choosing the yarns for your project is an exciting and important step. The decisions you make will be affected by your idea, the size of your weaving, techniques you will use, whether the project is decorative or functional, and how you want to use colour and texture. Here I want to give you some practical information on yarns. In 'Designing for weaving,' (p. 98) there is more about design and colour.

For the weaving techniques in this book, four types of yarn will be the most suitable and easiest to handle. All are natural, animal or vegetable fibres.

Cotton is a vegetable fibre which is very strong and washes well. For tapestry warp and for braid weaving.
Linen is hard-wearing but can be difficult to handle as its tension is affected by a moist atmosphere. For tapestry warp and braids.
Silk has a beautiful lustre, is strong but very expensive, so use for added interest in tapestry and for fine braids.

Wool is an animal fibre and the most resilient and popular. Wool is spun into either woollen or worsted yarn. Woollen yarn consists of the long and short fibres from the fleece, spiralled together when spun into a soft yarn. Worsted uses only the long fibres which are spun parallel to one another into a smooth strong yarn. Woollen yarns are used for tapestry and braid wefts, worsted is good for a braid warp and is also used for tapestry weft if stranded together.

Because you will spend some time on your weaving projects, it is important not only to choose the most suitable yarns but ones you like the look and feel of, in the best quality you can afford. The investment will pay off if you want to derive real satisfaction from the end product. The advantage of weaving without a loom is that you are saving considerably on equipment, so the main items you will be purchasing are the yarns.

I am often asked in classes if it is acceptable to use knitting yarns and I invariably say no. They have much more elasticity than weaving yarns and given an uneven, amateurish appearance to the weaving. There are, however, some fancy knitting yarns, such as mohair, bouclé and man-made metallic threads which can be used as weft in tapestry for added textural interest. Crochet cottons, both mercerised and corded, are good for backstrap and tablet braids.

Yarn terminology

Singles are fibres spun into one strand of yarn. They can be spun clockwise in an S twist, or anti-clockwise in a Z twist. Singles break easily so do not use as a warp.

Ply or **fold** denotes the number of singles twisted together, e.g. 2-ply is two strands twisted together.

Yarn count describes the thickness of a yarn and the length of fibre per kilo. The fixed weight system can be used with imperial or metric weights and measures (and is used in Britain, Europe and America) and numbers yarns according to the length per kilo (lb). Thus a fine yarn has more metres (yards) to the fixed weight than a thick yarn, so the count is higher, whereas a thick yarn has a low count. The ply is also included, e.g. 2/12's or 12/2's is a yarn in which two singles with a count of 12 are plied together.

Buying yarn

First see if there is a supplier near to you who sells handweaving yarns, and go and look at what is available. The majority of weaving yarns, however, are sold by mail order, so initially you will need to write away for samples. The minimum quantities you can order vary from one supplier to another; with some it might be ½ kilo (1 lb), or it may be 100 gr. (3½ oz). An adequate first order for an individual would be: ½ kilo (1 lb) of medium weight undyed 2-ply cotton for tapestry warp and braids; 100–200 gr. (3½–7 oz) each in assorted colours of 2-ply yarn for tapestry weft and braids; 100–200 gr. (3½–7 oz) each in assorted colours of 2/12's wool worsted—or ½ kilo (1 lb) undyed if you want to dye colours yourself—for tapestry weft; and 50 gr. (1¾ oz) in assorted colours of mercerised or corded cotton in a medium weight for braids. It's more practical and economical to order in larger quantities, so if you belong to a weaving guild or class, get together to make an order.

Yarn packaging

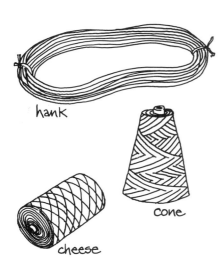

Hanks or skeins of yarn need to be wound off carefully before use. If you are dyeing your own colours, keep the yarn in hanks until you have finished dyeing, then put each hank around a chair, undo the tyeing cords and wind into balls.

A cheese, cop or spool is wound around a cardboard cylinder and needs to be placed on a stick or spool rack so that it can rotate as you wind off the yarn.

A cone of yarn, with a card cone at the centre, will stand on the table so winding off is easy.

Spools can be made from stiff, tightly-wound paper for holding small amounts of cotton or worsted.

hank

cone

cheese

spool

Diagram 2

Preparing the warp

Having selected the yarns you want to use for both warp and weft you will first of all need to prepare the warp. The simplest method is the one used for finger weaving, where lengths of yarn are measured off one and a half times the finished length, cut, and looped around a pencil. However, for braids which are much longer, especially with fine yarns which could tangle easily it is necessary to wind the warp around two fixed points and then transfer it to the weaving sticks, as in backstrap and tablet weaving (see pp. 26 and 36).

Two warping posts clamped to a table make an excellent, yet simple warping device (see p. 30). For backstrap weaving the warp is wound around the posts in a figure of eight, so the centre cross keeps the threads in the correct order. This is not essential for tablet weaving as the threads can be wound in colour groups until threaded through the tablets (Diag. 3). An alternative to warping posts is a warping frame with adjustable

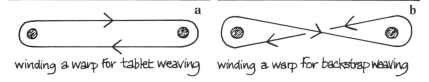

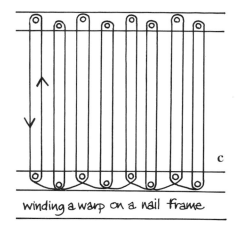

Warps a and b are in cross-section

a — winding a warp for tablet weaving

b — winding a warp for backstrap weaving

c — winding a warp on a nail frame

Diagram 3

pegs which enables you to wind a long warp without taking up much space (see p. 41). With a long warp it is wise to put three or four contrasting cords around it and to secure the cross before removing the warp from the posts or pegs on the frame.

Warping a tapestry does not require a separate warping device since you wind the warp straight onto the frame. The simplest method is to wind the warp continuously from top to bottom in a figure of eight (Diag. 4). On a nail frame the warp is wound around the nails (Diag. 3).

Tensioning the warp and spacing it

On a tapestry frame the tension of the warp must be kept firm and even as you wind it around the frame. Whether you are able to adjust the tension once you have begun weaving will depend on the type of frame you use. On the large frame on p. 55 the tension bolts can be adjusted to tighten or loosen the warp. On the smaller frames you cannot slacken the warp but it can be tightened by inserting two flat sticks at the top in opposite sheds.

The warp spacing on a frame is determined by marks or notches in the wood, or the nails, and this is calculated before you begin warping (see p. 55). The spacing depends on the thickness of weft and the degree of detail you want in the tapestry. Once you have warped up the frame, the spacing is maintained at the lower edge with a woven heading, a row of twining or half-hitch knots (pp. 56 and 57).

For backstrap and tablet weaving the warp is wound around two fixed points, then transferred onto two sticks which are stretched out in tension. One is attached to a firm post or door handle, or clamped to a table, and the other to the waist of the weaver. By leaning back or forwards slightly the weaver creates the tension needed in the warp to be able to weave (pp. 28 and 43). As both backstrap and tablet weaving are warp-faced, with the warp ends pushed closely together, a spacing method at the beginning of the warp is not necessary.

The warp is in cross-section

Winding a warp around a simple frame

Diagram 4

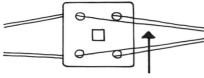

The warps are in cross-section

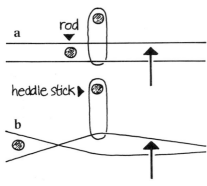

The shed in tablet weaving

a   rod

heddle stick ▸

b

The sheds in backstrap weaving

Diagram 5

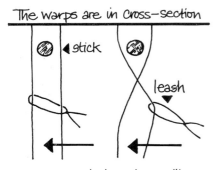

The warps are in cross-section

◂ stick

leash

The sheds in tapestry, with a stick and leashes

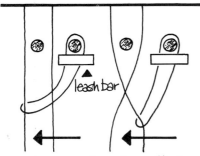

leash bar

The sheds in tapestry, with a stick and leashes attached to a bar

Making the sheds in the warp

The sheds are two V-shaped openings made in the warp between alternate warp ends, through which the weft is passed. Without sheds weaving would be rather slow, much like darning, so a means of opening the sheds is necessary to speed up the weaving.

In tablet weaving the sheds are created by the way the tablets are threaded. The warp ends through the upper holes automatically separate from those through the lower holes when the warp is in tension, so the weft can be passed through the opening (Diag. 5). As the tablets are turned, the threads change position, so the next shed automatically opens.

With backstrap weaving two sticks are inserted into the warp, through alternate sheds, called the rod and heddle stick. The shed made by the rod is always accessible (Diag. 5a). The opposite shed for the alternate row is made by attaching heddles round alternate warp ends and to another stick. The heddle stick has to be lifted up to open this shed (Diag. 5b). A flat batten, or shed stick, is inserted into each shed and turned on end to hold the shed open.

On a tapestry frame the sheds can be made with a rod and heddle stick or with a stick and leashes (Diag. 6). The leashes, like heddles, are made with loops of cotton and are pulled to open the shed. The two kinds of leashes are described on pp. 58 and 59.

With finger weaving there is no fixed device for opening the sheds. This is because all the threads can act as either warp or weft in different rows. On p. 19 I have described how to use a long needle to open the shed for each row, so the weft can be passed through the warp more easily.

Preparing the weft

Finger weaving doesn't need any weft preparation as all the threads act as both warp and weft at different stages in the weaving. In backstrap and tablet weaving the weft is usually the same type and colour as the selvedges of the warp. The weft can be wound into a butterfly, (see p. 59) or around a thin spool of paper, (see p. 12), small enough to be passed easily through the warp. For tapestry weaving, which requires a great number of wefts, each separate weft is wound in a butterfly. The yarn can be pulled out from the butterfly as the weaving progresses, and when not in use left hanging at the front of the weaving.

Diagram 6

Weaving the weft through the sheds in the warp, beating it down and keeping the correct tension

How the weft is inserted into the shed and beaten down depends on the type of weave structure. For a balanced weave, as in some types of finger weaving, the weft is inserted through the warp and beaten down gently so the warp and weft show equally. Care should be taken not to pull in the selvedges. Bunching of warp ends at the selvedges is a sign of a tight weft and slack warp ends.

For warp-faced weaves, as in backstrap and tablet weaving, the weft is pulled quite tightly through the shed, so the warp ends close together, and are then beaten towards the weaver firmly. Only the warp should be visible on the surface. I have described pulling the weft through from the previous row on pp. 33 and 44, rather than pulling it through in the open row, as this seems to help maintain straight edges.

Tapestry weave is a weft-faced weave, with a taut warp and wefts which are inserted loosely. The weft is made into a series of arcs in the open row which are then beaten down very firmly with a comb or fork. The weft must cover the warp completely, and if there are any signs of the warp showing and the weft not beating down easily, this is an indication that the weft is too tight or the warp is too slack.

Removing the weaving and finishing it

Finishing off the weaving is as important as making it and can make or mar the final appearance. Cutting the warp, securing the warp ends, finishing and darning in loose weft ends, and then deciding how to hang, mount, or make your weaving into a finished piece all require thought and patience. At the end of the braid and tapestry sections, I have outlined the main methods of finishing off, and included some suggestions on edgings and ways of hanging weaving.

Equipment

Braid and tapestry weaving need very little equipment and most of what you need you can make yourself. Apart from saving costs, weaving without a loom saves space and the work is easily portable. In each chapter on braid weaving I have given a list of the equipment you will need. In the tapestry section of the book, the first chapter explains what you need to make your own frame.

Finger weaving

Introduction

Let's begin at the beginning with finger weaving. This is probably the earliest type of weaving, so called because the fingers of the weaver were the only tools used to manipulate the threads. It was originally a technique for making narrow braids which could be worn as belts or sashes, or used as straps for tying and carrying everyday items. As more decorative patterns were developed, finger woven braids became a distinctive part of ceremonial costume.

From the research which has been done on early textiles it seems that the cultures which developed the techniques of finger weaving most were those of Ancient Peru and the North American Indians. The skills those early weavers used to make such beautifully patterned braids show us how much can be achieved with the simple use of a few threads.

So let's define finger weaving. It is a technique in which one thread, acting as a weft, is taken over and under the other threads, acting as the warp, to make a row of weaving. But as each row changes so the threads which act as the warp and weft change. The patterns in the weave come about by arranging the colours and weaving the threads in a particular sequence. Finger weaving is nearly always in plain weave, and the weave structure can be a balanced or a warp-faced weave (see p. 8). The unusual feature of finger weaving is that it uses all the threads as warp and weft, unlike other forms of weaving where the warp and weft threads are distinctly separate elements. If you were to unpick your finger woven braid you would only have a bundle of threads. If you unpicked your tablet or backstrap woven braid you would have a group of warp threads in tension and a weft thread or threads. The important thing to remember about finger weaving is that the role of the threads is flexible, that is to say each thread does not act only as warp or weft, but can become one or the other.

North American Indian finger woven braid. Courtesy of the Museum of Mankind, the British Museum.

Colour plate:
Weaving braids and tapestries requires little equipment. Some pieces of wood, tablets and a selection of yarns are all you need to start.

When you begin a finger woven braid, you have a number of threads laid parallel to one another in a particular colour sequence. In the first row one (or more) threads act as the weft, and they are interlaced through the remaining threads which act as the warp. In the next and succeeding rows this sequence will change, as the weft from the previous row will be dropped parallel with the other threads to become part of the warp again, and a new thread is picked up as the weft.

All the braids in this section are in plain weave.

Preparation and materials

Although finger weaving needs only some threads and the dexterity of your fingers, the following items will be useful and enable you to weave with greater ease:

A piece of softboard approx. 25 × 35 cm (10 × 14 in)
Dressmaking pins
A pencil
A knitting needle or long carpet needle
A large bulldog clip
Scissors
A tape measure
Assorted coloured weaving yarns in approx. 25–50 gr. (1–2 oz) quantities, such as 2-ply rug yarn, tightly spun weaving yarn, tapestry wool, corded or mercerised cotton.

For your first finger woven braids you may find it easier to work with rug yarns. As you become more proficient, experiment with other threads, for example, use cotton for delicate narrow braids, or weave with furnishing cords or ribbons. If you use woollen yarn, the most successful is a tightly spun wool because it gives a good firm feel to the finished braid. If you find it difficult to buy, here are two methods you can try, to re-spin it yourself.

Finger woven braids (colour)
Left to right: **1** Diagonal striped braid   **2** Peruvian diagonal weave braid   **3** Peruvian repp braid, zig-zag pattern   **4** Peruvian repp braid, chevron pattern   **5** Peruvian repp braid, cross pattern   **6** American Indian braid, arrowhead pattern. Woven by the author.

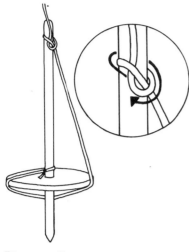

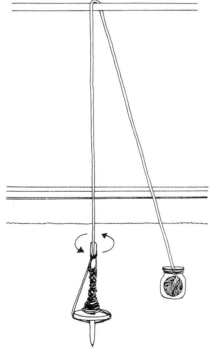

Diagram 7

Diagram 8

Re-spinning purchased yarns

You need a spindle to do this, inexpensive and available from weaving suppliers. Put your ball of yarn in a jar, take the end and hang it over something high up so you can spin good long lengths at a time. Attach the end to the shaft of the spindle with two half-hitches (Diag. 7). Let the spindle hang just above the floor and spin it so that the yarn is turning in the same direction as the twist already in the yarn (Diag. 8). The resulting yarn will be firmly and tightly spun. Undo the hitch, wind the re-spun yarn around the shaft, tie the yarn to the spindle and spin again.

Double-twisting purchased yarns

This method is more suitable for softer tapestry wools than the previous method. Cut the woollen threads twice the finished length you need for the braid; this is to allow for take-up as you weave. Each thread must be double, not single, so to do this knot a pair of threads together at one end and hook them to something firm. Take one thread at the free end, hold it taut, twist very tightly in one direction, (it doesn't matter which) and weight it down under something heavy. Do the same with the other thread, twisting it in the *same* direction as the first. Pick up both threads and twist them very tightly together in the *opposite* direction. Knot the ends and weave as a single thread.

Setting up threads for weaving

First of all you need to estimate the length of the braid you want to weave, as well as allowing approximately 18 cm (7 in) for fringes. A good rule of thumb guide is to cut the threads $1\frac{1}{2}$ times the complete finished length. This will allow for take-up during weaving. Cut the number of threads according to the instructions which follow: this will vary depending on the braid you choose to make. The centre of each length is then looped around a pencil (Diag. 9) in the order given in the instructions. Starting to weave in the middle of the threads means you avoid working with very long strands which could get tangled, and your pattern will be centred nicely on the braid.

Arrange the threads on the pencil in the order given, and tie an overhand knot in all the threads above the pencil. Pin the knot to the board and also secure the pencil with pins above and below it. Sort out the threads so they are neat and parallel to one another. Start just below the pencil and follow the weaving instructions. As you progress you will no doubt find your own way of manipulating the threads and it will become easier, but here are a few tips which might help.

With quite a number of threads it may seem a little difficult at first to make the shed with your fingers, especially on warp-faced weaves where you are easing the threads closely together. I find it helps a great deal to use a knitting needle or carpet needle at least 15 cm (6 in) long as a pick.

Feed this over and under the warp threads in each row, holding it up to open the shed so you can pass the weft through with your other hand.

It also seems easier to weave if the warp threads are held in tension, (the weft thread having been separated and left loose, of course.) I use a bulldog clip to do this, clipping it to the bottom edge of the board with the warp threads trapped in it. After the weft has been passed through the shed of one row, remove the clip, tighten your weft, then drop it parallel with the warp. Release the next weft thread and clip the remaining warp threads to the board (Diag. 10 and photo below).

Finally, always use pins liberally. They will help to keep everything in place and will also help you to keep the braid straight, particularly on diagonally woven patterns which tend to distort and shift to one side. Very lightly steam pressing a distorted braid, having blocked it out on the ironing board with pins first, will also help to straighten a braid.

The diagrams for the braids on the following pages do not show the exact number of threads as indicated in the text, but are meant to serve as a guide for the method of weaving.

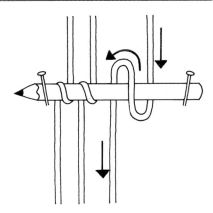

Diagram 9

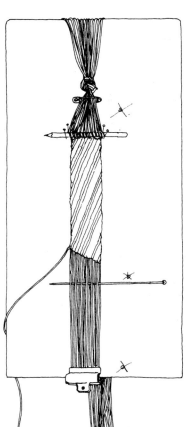

Diagram 10

Mount the threads onto a pencil and pin them to a piece of soft-board to make weaving easier. Keep the wefts separate and clamp the rest, which act as the warp, to the edge of the board with a bull-dog clip.

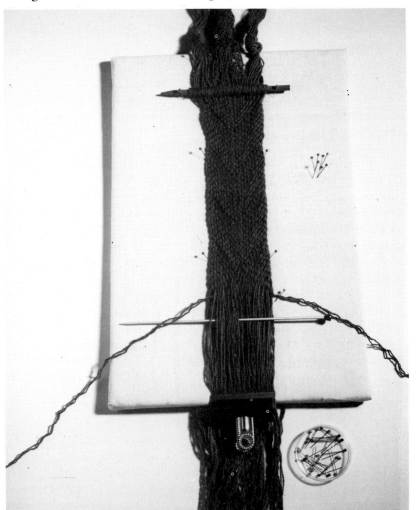

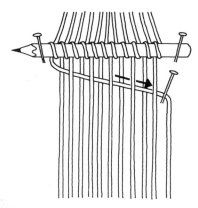

Diagram 11

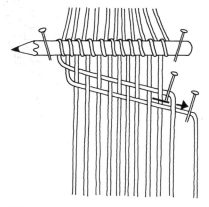

Diagram 12

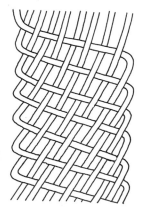

Diagram 13

Diagonal striped braid

The striking diagonally striped pattern in this braid originates from the American Indian sashes. It is woven in plain weave, with a balanced weave structure. The different coloured threads running across and down show equally, giving a plaid effect, (see photo facing p. 17). Try weaving this braid first before you attempt the other patterns.

Cut 6 threads in colour A, 6 threads in B, 6 threads in C, and 3 threads in D, each 2.25 metres (2¼ yds) long.

Arrange the threads on the pencil from left to right in the following order: 3A/3B/3C/3D/3C/3B/3A. Pin the threads to the board.

Begin by separating the far left A thread. Clip the remaining 20 threads to the bottom edge of the board. Take the A thread, acting as the weft in this row, and pass it over and under each warp thread alternately towards the right using your fingers or a needle to make the shed. Release the clip, pull the weft slightly until the warp and weft are evenly balanced. Put a pin just below the weft and let it drop parallel with the other threads (Diag. 11).

Now separate the far left A thread (the second thread in the original order.) Clip the remaining 20 threads to the board, including the right A thread which was your weft in the last row. Weave a second row, taking your new weft through the opposite shed to the first row (Diag. 12). These two rows are then repeated continuously, and each time you transfer the far right thread from being a weft back into the group of warp threads and release the far left thread so it becomes the new weft (Diag. 13).

Use the pins to keep the threads in place as you need to, and to help keep the edges straight. Because you are constantly weaving from left to right the braid will distort and pull to the right, so pinning is essential.

When you have woven as far as you can, having left a fringe allowance of approximately 9 cm (3½ in), turn the board around, untie the knot and remove the pencil. Pull out the loops and straighten the threads on the board. Weave this half of the braid exactly as before. For fringes, see finishing techniques, pp. 50 and 51. This braid is shown in photo facing p. 17.

Peruvian diagonal weave braid

This is a nice simple braid, originating from one of the earliest techniques used by the weavers of Ancient Peru. The weft in each row progresses from the right to the left edge. (You can weave from left to right if you find it easier.) This braid is in a balanced weave, so make sure the warp and weft threads show equally. If you pull the weft too tightly, the warp threads will close up. You always need an odd number of threads for this braid.

For a braid of a finished length of 1.50 metres (1⅔ yds), cut 2 threads in colour A, 3 threads in B, and 2 threads in C, each 2.25 metres (2½ yds) long.

Arrange the threads on the pencil from left to right in the following order: 2A/3B/2C. Pin the threads to the board.

Pick up the outer right C thread and weave it under the next two threads C and B, over the next B thread, under the third B thread and over the last two A threads. Secure the weft with pins at the right and left of the threads, then drop it back parallel with the warp on the left (Diag. 14). Pick up the outer right C thread and weave it under the next two B threads, over one B thread, under one A thread and over the last two threads A and C. Drop this weft down on the left (Diag. 15). As you will see, you always take the weft under the first two threads, over then under the centre two threads and over the last two threads (Diag. 16). If you set up more threads for a wider braid, the weaving sequence still remains under the first two, then over and under repeatedly in the centre group, and over the last two threads. Because you are constantly weaving from right to left your braid will tend to shift to one side. Correct this by pinning the threads on every row and adjusting the tension to straighten the braid.

When you have woven as far as you can, turn the board around, remove the pencil, and weave the second half of the braid, except that now you take the outer right thread and weave it over the first two threads, under then over, and under the last two. Continue each row like this. For fringes, see finishing techniques pp. 50 and 51. This braid is shown in the photo facing p. 17.

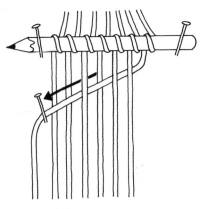

Diagram 14

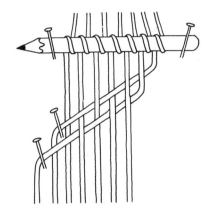

Diagram 15

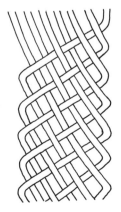

Diagram 16

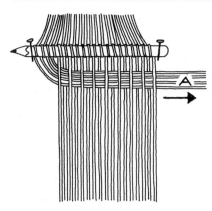

Diagram 17

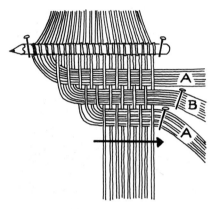

Diagram 18

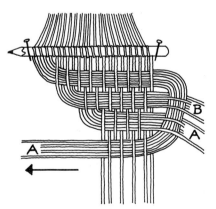

Diagram 19

Peruvian repp braid, zig-zag pattern

By 300 AD the weavers of Ancient Peru were making intricate finger woven patterns that have not been found elsewhere, such was their development of the skill. One of the techniques they devised was to weave warp and weft threads through one another in groups rather than singly. The result of this was that some coloured threads could completely cover others, or be covered themselves, and this enabled the weaver to create very intricate designs. The three braids I have chosen here all have a thicker, ribbed type of weave as the weft threads are passed through the warp in groups of four. This weave is called repp.

For a braid of finished length of 1.50 metres (1⅔ yds), cut 12 threads in colour A, 6 threads in colour B and 12 threads in C, each 2.25 metres (2½ yds) long.

Arrange the threads on the pencil from right to left in the following order: 4A/4B/4A/6C/2A/2B/2A/6C. Pin the threads to the board.

This braid is in a warp-faced weave, so pull the wefts through firmly and ease the warp threads closely together. Separate the four outer left A threads, and taking them in a group as one weft, pass them over and under each of the 26 warp threads. Place them on the right edge of the weaving parallel with the pencil (Diag. 17). Take the four outer left B threads as one weft and pass them through the 22 warp threads in the opposite shed. Lay this group below and parallel with the first group. Pick up the four outer left A threads and repeat, taking them through 18 warp threads, so you now have three grouped wefts, A, B and A lying at the right of the weaving (Diag. 18). Put a pin just below each of the last two groups, A and B, and drop them so they are parallel with the warp again. Take the top far right group of A threads and weave them to the left over and under the 26 threads. Place them parallel with the pencil on the left edge of the weaving (Diag. 19). Repeat with the next group of B threads, weaving them through the 22 warp threads, and then the last group of A threads, weaving them through 18 warp threads.

You now have all the threads back in their original order. Repeat the whole sequence, moving the three groups of wefts continuously from left to right and back again. Turn the braid around as already described on p. 20 and weave the other half. For fringes, see finishing techniques, pp. 50 and 51. This braid is shown in photo facing p. 17.

Peruvian repp braid, chevron pattern

This braid is in a warp-faced weave, so pull your weft threads through the shed firmly so the warp threads close together. Like the previous braid this is also woven with grouped wefts through single warp threads.

For a braid of finished length of 1.50 metres ($1\frac{2}{3}$ yds), cut 16 threads in colour A, 8 threads in B, 16 threads in C and 8 threads in D, each 2.25 metres ($2\frac{1}{2}$ yds) long, 48 threads in all.

Arrange the threads on the pencil from left to right in the following order: 4A/4B/4A/4C/4D/8C/4D/4C/4A/4B/4A. Pin the threads to the board.

Begin by taking the outer left four A threads in a group as one weft and weaving them over and under single warp threads as far as the centre (Diag. 20). Then take the four outer right A threads and weave them over and under single warp threads to the centre. Now cross the centre eight A threads by making a shed in the left of centre four A threads and pass the right of centre A threads through it (Diag. 21).

Continue weaving each outer left and then right group of wefts into the centre, and crossing the corresponding coloured groups at the centre as already described. The result is a chevron pattern which repeats the length of the braid (Diag. 22).

After you have woven one half of the braid, pull out the pencil, straighten the loops and begin the second half. First cross the two centre groups of four C threads by weaving the right of centre group through the shed in the left of centre group. Now weave the outer left group of four A threads to the centre, and the outer right group of A threads to the centre, cross them, and continue exactly as for the first half of the braid. The pattern at the centre of the braid will form a cross, with the chevron inverted in the second half.

For fringes, see finishing techniques, pp. 50 and 51. This braid is shown in the photo facing p. 17.

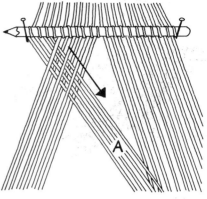

Diagram 20

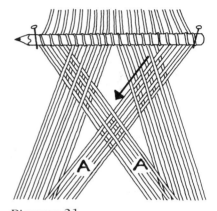

Diagram 21

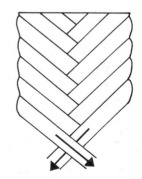

Diagram 22

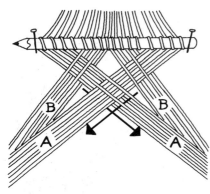

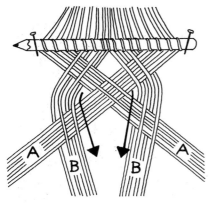

Diagram 23

Peruvian repp braid, cross pattern

For a braid of finished length of 1.50 metres (1⅔ yds) cut 8 threads in colour A and 8 threads in B, each 2.25 metres (2½ yds) long.

Arrange the threads on the pencil from left to right in the following order: 4A/8B/4A. Pin the threads to the board.

Pick up the outer left four A threads and weave them as one weft group over and under the first four B threads, then leave them just left of centre. Pick up the outer right four A threads and weave them as one weft over and under the four B threads right of centre, then through the four A threads already placed at the centre, so you have made a cross with the eight centre A threads (Diag. 23).

Now you need to cross the B threads. Make a shed, opposite to the last row, in the left group of four B threads and weave the centre left four A threads through it to the left edge of the braid. Do the same on the right, by weaving the centre right four A threads through a shed in the right group of four B threads towards the right edge of the braid (Diag. 24).

Complete the weaving sequence by crossing the centre B threads. Make a shed in the left of centre group of four B threads and pass the right of centre group through it (Diag. 25). All the threads are now back in their original positions. Repeat the pattern throughout the weaving. Weave the second half of the braid by turning the board around, removing the pencil and continuing as already described on p. 20.

For fringes, see finishing techniques, pp. 50 and 51. This braid is shown in photo facing p. 17.

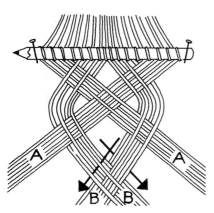

Diagram 24

Diagram 25

American Indian braid, arrowhead pattern

Finally, back to the Indian braiding but with a variation. This braid is in a balanced weave, using single warp and weft threads and an interlocking technique.

For a braid of finished length of 1.50 metres, (1⅔ yds), cut 22 threads in colour A and 18 threads in B, each 2.25 metres (2½ yds) long.

Arrange the threads on the pencil from left to right in the following order: 11A/18B/11A. Pin the threads to the board.

The wefts in this pattern start at the centre and move outwards to the left and right. Find the centre two B threads and separate the left and right groups.

Pick up the left of centre B thread and weave it through the shed towards the right, until you reach the ninth A thread counting from the centre. Interlock the A and B threads and drop the B thread back into the warp. Now pick up the ninth A thread as a weft and weave it through the shed to the right edge through the last two A threads. Repeat with the right of centre B thread taking it over the B thread you have just woven, and through the shed towards the left until it reaches the ninth A thread counting from the centre. Interlock the A and B threads, drop the B thread and continue with the A thread through the shed to the left edge (Diag. 26).

Now begin the second row with the left of centre B thread as a weft, weaving it through the opposite shed, but this time taking it only as far as the eighth A thread. Interlock the A and B thread then weave the A thread through the last three threads to the right. Pick up the right of centre B thread, cross it over the left of centre B thread, then weave through the shed to the eighth A thread. Interlock A and B, and continue with A through the last three threads to the left. You have now interlocked twice on each row, and the tip of the arrowhead is beginning to show. Continue weaving, but on each row you successively interlock the seventh, sixth, fifth, fourth, third, second and first A threads at the right and left sides of each row. Always remember to cross the centre B threads at the start of each row (Diag. 27).

After every row adjust the tension of all the threads so the arrowhead pattern is clearly defined. You may also need to tighten the interlocked threads a little. When you have completed nine rows your threads will be back in their original positions.

Begin the weaving sequence again with the centre two B threads. When you have woven the first half of the braid, turn the board around, remove the pencil, straighten out the loops and weave the second half exactly as the first. The arrowhead will automatically reverse in the second half of the braid. For fringes, see finishing techniques, pp. 50 and 51. This braid is shown in the photo facing p. 17.

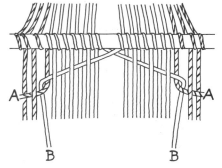

Diagram 26

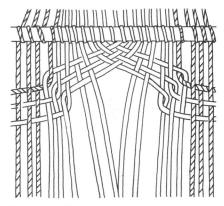

Diagram 27

Diagram 28

Backstrap weaving

Introduction

It is extraordinary to think what little equipment the weavers in earlier civilisations needed to produce beautiful textiles. Of all the methods first used to produce woven textiles, the backstrap loom has probably been the most widely used. To quote from Eric Broudy's *The book of looms*, '. . . some of the world's finest weaving has been done on a tool as crude as the backstrap loom.'

The parts of the backstrap loom may seem crude to us, often no more than pieces of bamboo, reed, or branches finely honed into shape, but the weaver brought skill and ingenuity to the process and the intricately patterned textiles which have survived are an inspiration to the modern weaver.

Backstrap weaving is one of the oldest and most portable means of weaving narrow bands of cloth, and is still being carried on in some areas today. The earliest backstrap looms consisted of two sticks to hold the warp, which were stretched in tension between the waist of the weaver and a nearby post or tree. Additional sticks were then inserted into the warp to enable the weft to be passed through and to create patterns in the weave. Many variations of this method of weaving have been discovered worldwide and they are so diverse that it would seem that backstrap weaving did not have a common origin, but was in fact 'invented' more than once by primitive peoples as a simple and effective way of producing cloth.

Evidence of backstrap woven braids and narrow cloth, as well as parts of the looms, have been found in north-west India, China, Japan, Tibet, Malaysia, Indonesia, and the Pacific, as well as in Africa and South America, particularly Peru, Mexico and Guatemala. The tradition still continues today in some of these areas. In Peru narrow, striped bands of cloth, using wool and alpaca, are woven to make ponchos and blankets, and in Mexico and Guatemala brilliantly coloured, brocaded patterned braids, using motifs distinctive to each village, are woven for the traditional Indian costumes.

The backstrap loom

The backstrap loom is a very simple tool used for weaving narrow bands of cloth (Diag. 29) but don't think of the description 'loom' in the modern sense of the word. The warp on the backstrap loom is simply stretched between two sticks. One stick, or 'beam' as it is called, is attached to a fixed point such as a door handle and the other beam to a backstrap worn around the waist or hips of the weaver. Backstrap weaving was traditionally carried out by women and this is still mainly the case today. Once the weaver has set up her warp she then weaves her cloth in either a sitting, kneeling or standing position, always keeping the warp very taut. The threads, colours and patterns she uses will all be indigenous to her region and the woven fabric will be used for a particular purpose, usually as part of traditional dress.

If you are a beginner to weaving, or want to get away from your loom and try some traditional methods of producing cloth or braids, you will find that there are many advantages with the backstrap loom. It is easy to assemble, can be carried and set up anywhere and folded up when not in use so that it takes up no more space than a piece of knitting or embroidery.

Backstrap looms vary, but there are basic sticks which are common to all. Look at Diag. 29. The back and front sticks, or beams (a) hold the warp, with an additional stick at the front, called a 'cloth-beam,' around which the braid is rolled as weaving progresses. Two more sticks are threaded through the warp to make the alternate sheds for plain weaving. One is the rod which makes the stick shed (b), the other is the heddle stick (c), with loops or heddles of cotton attached to it, which makes the pull shed. The final stick, called the batten (d), is flat and smooth and holds the shed open so the weft can be inserted, and also acts as a beater for the weft. A stretcher (e), is also useful, usually a piece of bamboo about 1.25 cm ($\frac{1}{2}$ in) thick, with two small pins which are pushed into each end at points which are the same width as your braid. This is hooked behind the weaving as it progresses to help you maintain an even width.

To set up the warp you also need some strong cord and a backstrap, which can either be a leather belt or a woven braid (f). Your first project could be to weave a braid for your backstrap. The weft can be wound into a butterfly or around a narrow tube of paper (g).

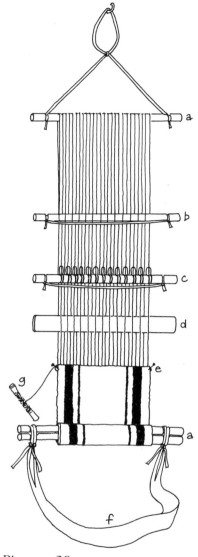

Diagram 29

What you can weave on a backstrap loom

Backstrap woven fabrics can vary in width from about 2.5 cm (1 in) to 75 cm (30 in), and in length up to about 5 metres ($5\frac{1}{2}$ yds). Anything wider or longer than this becomes difficult to operate, so traditionally backstrap weaving has been used for braids, or narrow bands of cloth which were then joined together. As a result clothes made in this way have always consisted of rectangular uncut pieces of cloth, for example the huipils made by the women of Guatemala which are worn as loose-fitting blouses. You may not start by making a huipil, but there are many things that backstrap weaving can be used for.

Sashes, belts, cummerbunds and braids are simple, as well as little neck-purses, larger carrier bags, ties, and straps for bags, guitars or for hanging things such as plants. For furnishing, braids can be stitched together to make cushions or to edge ready-made ones and to decorate blinds or lampshades (see p. 108). For your first backstrap braid try weaving something 5 cm (2 in) wide and about a metre or yard long, to practise the techniques.

Preparation and materials

The warp

Traditionally backstrap fabrics have been woven in very fine cotton or wool. For your first attempt try a medium thickness cotton thread which is smooth and strong, so you won't be daunted by too many warp threads and also so your warp won't stick to the heddles while you are weaving. Warp threads can be waxed or sized before starting to weave. Rub beeswax on the warp or, as the Guatemalan women do, make a solution of flour and hot water (1 tablespoon to 1 gallon of water), allow to cool, dip your warp into it and let it dry. A woollen warp must dry completely whereas a cotton warp can be woven while still slightly damp.

For your first braid it is probably best to start with a plain or simple striped warp in a medium thickness cotton. To estimate the number of threads per 2.5 cm (1 in), wind the warp around a ruler across 2.5 cm (1 in), so that between each thread there is a space of half the thickness of the thread. Let us say there are 14 threads, for example. For a 5 cm (2 in) braid you will need 28 threads plus two, so the selvedge warp threads are double. Estimate the length of braid you want to weave and add on half as much again to allow for take up in the weaving; for example, for a 1 metre (1 yd) braid, wind the warp 1.5 metres (1½ yds) long.

The weft

Backstrap weaving is usually a warp-faced weave, although it can be a balanced weave. The very decorative South American braids have a warp-faced plain or striped ground with floating wefts in thicker threads added which make the patterns; this is called 'brocading'. So for the weft use the same type and thickness of thread as the warp for plain woven braids and for ground weave. For the supplementary wefts in brocaded patterns, use doubled thread or a much thicker thread than the warp.

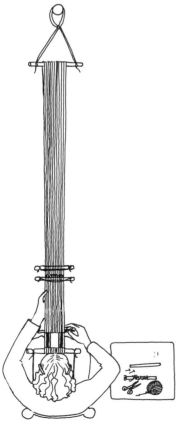

Diagram 30

Other equipment

I have described the equipment you will need on p. 27. The wooden sticks, which are the main tools needed for backstrap weaving, should all be a length which equals the width of the braid you want to weave plus about 15 cm (6 in). For example, to weave a braid 5 cm (2 in) wide cut all the sticks 20 cm (8 in) long. You will need:

5 sticks made from 1.25 cm ($\frac{1}{2}$ in) wooden dowel (round)
1 stick made from 2 cm × 0.5 cm ($\frac{3}{4}$ in × $\frac{1}{4}$ in) wooden baton (flat)
1 stick made from 1.25 cm ($\frac{1}{2}$ in) bamboo, with two tiny holes made in it 5 cm (2 in) apart.

Cut a groove at each end of the pieces of dowel, about 2.5 cm (1 in) from the edges. This will stop the tying cords from slipping off the sticks. Sandpaper the batten so it is very smooth.

To wind the warp for backstrap weaving you will also need a pair of G clamps and two single warping posts. The latter can be bought from weaving suppliers, but it is easy to make your own. Cut two 15 cm (6 in) lengths of 2.5 cm (1 in) wooden dowel and two pieces of wood, 7.5 cm (3 in) square by 2.5 cm (1 in) thick. Drill a hole right through the wood in the centre and also drill a little way into each piece of dowel at one end only. Glue and screw the dowel and base together with 5 cm (2 in) screws (Diag. 31 on p. 30).

A backstrap loom set up for weaving. The weaver is from Nagaland, N. India. Courtesy of the Serpentine Gallery, London (Arts Council of Great Britain). Photo: Roger Perry.

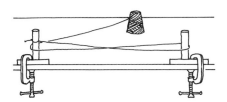

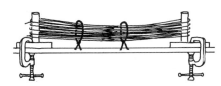

Diagram 31

Setting up backstrap weaving

Winding a plain warp

Position the warping posts 1.5 metres (1½ yds) apart on a table and clamp them in place. Tie the warp to one post and wind it continuously around both posts in a figure of eight (Diag 31). Each complete turn around both posts will make two warp ends. Count the warp in the middle where the threads cross until you have 30 warp ends in total. Tie the end of the warp to the post. Tie two brightly coloured threads (cross-ties) loosely through the warp at either side of the cross (Diag. 31); this is to keep the warp threads in the correct sequence.

Winding a striped warp

You can make a vertically striped warp by knotting together different coloured threads at the posts, as you wind around them. The narrowest stripe you can make is with two warp ends, so you must wind a complete round of both posts with one colour. Knot a new colour to the previous one with a half-hitch, making sure your knots are at the outside of each post so the joins will come at the very top and bottom edges of the warp when transferred to the beams of the loom.

You can also wind a multi-coloured warp which will create horizontal stripes when woven. Alternate two coloured threads every half round so you are changing colour at each post. Do this at least four times with two colours. When you weave, only one colour will show in the weave in one row and the other colour in the next row, and this appears as horizontal stripes. Different coloured threads for a striped warp are wound in a figure of eight around the posts exactly as for a plain warp, with cross-ties added when complete.

You now need to transfer the warp from the warping posts onto the beams of the loom. At this stage check carefully that your warp has an even tension throughout. Sometimes the posts can lean inwards with the tension of the warp, so your last threads are tighter than your first. Look at this now and correct it if necessary, or you will have difficulty weaving on an uneven warp.

Attaching the warp to the beams of the backstrap loom

Take two of the round sticks which will be the front and back beams, and slide them inside the warp at each end alongside the warping posts. With great care ease the warp off the posts and onto the beams, and gently place the warp flat on the table. Tie a loop of strong cord to the back beam and make a loop in the centre. Hang your warp up by the loop to something firm such as a door-handle or a hook.

Gather all the weaving equipment around you within easy reach, including the other sticks, the backstrap, and your warp and weft threads. Tie two lengths of cord to each end of your backstrap and put it around your waist or hips. Pick up the warp by the front beam and tie the cords to each end of it. Gradually ease yourself back until the warp is straight and taut (Diag. 30).

The rod and heddle sticks

Two sticks are now inserted into the warp so you can make the sheds for plain weaving. First lift up the cross-tie furthest from you. Pass one stick, now called the rod, through the space made by the cross-tie between the upper and lower layers of the warp. Remove the cross-tie. Tie a thread from one end of the rod to the other, over the warp, so that it is secure.

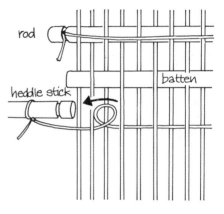

Lift the other cross-tie and pass the batten through the warp in the same space. Remove this cross-tie. You are now going to make the heddles, which are loops of cotton attached between the other stick and the alternate warp threads behind the rod you already have put in the warp. First, pass the end from a ball of cotton through the shed from right to left alongside the batten. Tie the end to the other stick, now called the heddle stick, with a slip knot, and hold it to the left side of the warp. Moving the stick in front of the warp, pull a loop in the cotton between the first and second warp threads lying on top of the batten (Diag. 32). Twist the loop and ease the stick through it.

Diagram 32

Pull another loop in the same place but anti-clockwise this time, and slip the stick through it. Pull the loop (heddle) tight. Whatever the thickness of your rod, the length of your heddles should measure slightly more, so that the shed made by the rod can pass through the heddles to the front of the warp when you are weaving. Make the second heddle by pulling the cotton in the space between the second and third warp threads lying on top of the batten (Diag. 33). Gradually move the heddle stick across the front of the warp as you attach each heddle to it. To finish, take more of the cotton left after the last heddle and pass it across the front of the stick and tie it to the other end, so the stick is securely held to the warp. Take out the batten.

To make a fringe allowance of about 7.5 cm (3 in) at the beginning of the warp, cut a strip of paper that width and pass it through alternate warp threads and pull it close to the front beam.

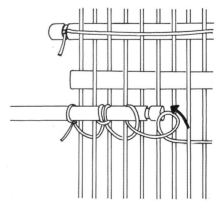

Diagram 33

Weaving on the backstrap loom

Plain weaving

Your weft should be the same coloured thread as the edges of the warp. Wind some weft into a butterfly (Diag. 68, p. 59) or around a thin tube of paper.

Sit upright so you maintain the tension of the warp. Lift the heddle stick so that it opens the pull shed (Diag. 34). It will help if you hold the batten in your other hand and press it down on the warp *behind* the heddle stick until the upper and lower threads of the warp separate. Alternatively, flick the end of the batten across the warp behind the heddles, whilst still lifting up the heddle stick. Using the side of your hand, ease open the shed towards you and put the batten in and turn it on end. Pass the weft through the shed from right to left and beat it towards you with the batten.

For the second shed, bring the rod down the warp towards you until it is immediately behind the heddle stick. This will make the opposite shed open, in front of the heddle stick, which is called the stick shed (Diag. 35). Flick the end of the batten across the warp in *front* of the heddle stick to help separate the upper and lower threads. Put the batten into this shed, turn it on end, pass the weft through from left to right and beat it towards you.

Because we want a warp-faced weave, the weft needs to be pulled through firmly so it holds the warp threads closely together. I find it easier to maintain an even width in the weaving if I leave a small loop of weft sticking out at the end of each row. Beat the weft firmly, change the shed for the next row, and before passing the weft through again, pull it until the loop draws in from the previous row.

So the sequence of weaving is:

Row 1   Lift the heddle stick, open the pull shed, pass the weft through from right to left, leaving a loop at the edge, and beat the weft towards you.

Row 2   Change to the stick shed and hold it open with the batten. Pull the loop in from the last row. Pass the weft through from left to right, and beat the weft towards you.

Left and right: Warp striped braids from Ecuador. The warp arrangement for these may probably have been a more intricate version of the striped braid on p. 35, using very fine multi-coloured threads.

Backstrap woven braids (colour)
Left to right: **1** Braid from Ecuador with multi-coloured warp **2** Braid woven by author, see p. 35 **3** Braid from Guatemala, with brocaded wefts **4** Brocaded braid woven by the author, see p. 35 **5** Simple warp-striped braid from India **6** Simple warp-striped braid from Guatemala.

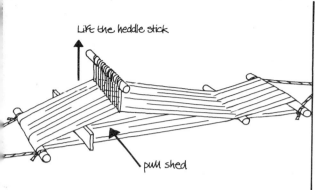

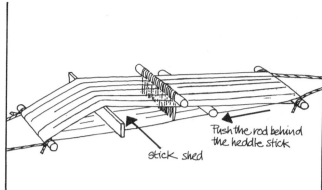

Diagram 34   Diagram 35

These two alternating rows are plain weave. Always remember that you can increase or slacken the tension of the warp by leaning forwards or back.

As your weaving progresses, you will find it more difficult to reach and will need to roll up some of the braid. Put your extra stick, the cloth beam, on top of the weaving next to the front beam. Roll up the weaving around both beams and re-tie the cords of the backstrap, first to the cloth-beam, then between each beam and finally around both several times.

The stretcher should be hooked to the back of the weaving near the top edge to help you keep an even width. Every so often you may need to clean the fuzz from the warp which builds up on the heddles. Carefully pick it off with the point of a needle or tiny scissors, but take great care not to cut or split either the heddles or the warp. This problem can be avoided by sizing or waxing the warp (p. 28) and by making sure that the threads you use for the warp and the heddles are smooth, such as corded or mercerised cotton. I wouldn't recommend a wool warp if you are a beginner, but if at some later point you want to use wool make sure it is smooth and tightly spun, (a wool worsted is the best choice), and size it before you begin weaving. If any warp threads break, then knot a new thread to the broken one with a double hitch knot at the weaving line, and carry it to the back beam and tie it securely. See p. 50 for darning in broken warp ends.

As your weaving reaches the back beam, you may have to remove the shed sticks and weave with a needle. Allow about 7.5 cm (3 in) of unwoven warp for fringes. To finish the weaving, cut the warp from the beams and knot, twist or plait the ends into decorative fringes (see pages 50 and 51). Darn any ends of weft across the braid alongside another weft.

Tablet woven braids (colour)
Top left to bottom right: **1** Black and white braid, see p. 46, variation 4 **2** Braid 2, see p. 47   **3** Braid 1, see p. 47   **4** Braid 3, see p. 48 **5** Braid 4, see p. 48   **6** Braid 5, see p. 49   **7** Black and white braid. see p. 46 variation 3. Woven by the author.

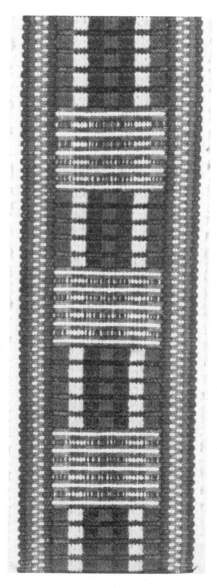

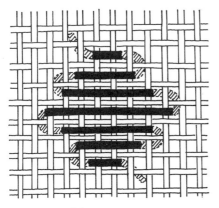

Diagram 36

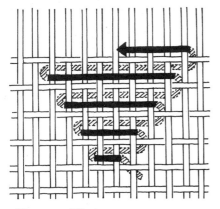

Diagram 37

Brocading

More elaborately patterned weaves can be made by introducing additional wefts, and this is known as brocading. The pattern wefts are thicker threads which are introduced into the warp in between the plain woven rows of the ground weft to make a highly decorated fabric. Brocading therefore uses several wefts; the ground weft which is the same thickness and type of thread as the warp, and the pattern wefts which are doubled or much thicker threads. The traditional brocaded weaves from Guatemala and Mexico are so colourful and intricate that they are often mistaken for embroidery. There are a number of different types of brocading but I will just describe two here. In both cases the pattern wefts are inserted into the warp with the sheds closed.

Overlay or two-faced brocading

In this method the pattern weft is carried over a number of warp ends on the front of the weaving and then passes under the next ground weft until it is needed again (Diag. 36). This makes a reversed pattern on the back of the weaving. The ends of the pattern weft can either be introduced into the warp with the previous ground weft and then tucked back in the same way, or can be darned in across the pattern on the back later.

The basic plain woven ground is made with the continuous ground weft being passed through the rod and heddle sheds alternately in the normal way, but between each row the pattern weft is brought to the front of the weaving and carried across the required number of warp ends and then put to the back. Because the pattern weft is much thicker it will almost cover the ground weave completely in areas of dense pattern. Use a separate butterfly of yarn for each of the different coloured pattern wefts and bring them to the front as you need them.

Wrapped or double-faced brocading

This method gives an identical pattern on both sides of the weave. The pattern weft is carried over a number of warp ends on the front, then passed through the warp to the back and across the same number of warp ends, so it is virtually being wrapped around groups of warp ends front and back (Diag. 37). The ground weft is woven through the alternate sheds between each pattern weft, as in overlay brocading.

Brocaded backstrap braid with additional wefts in stranded cottons. The pattern chart for this braid is on p. 35. Woven by the author.

Striped backstrap braid

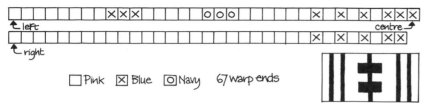

☐ Pink ☒ Blue ◯ Navy   67 warp ends

This is a simple braid with warp-faced stripes, woven in fine mercerised cotton (see photo). The pattern is made by the arrangement of different coloured warp threads as shown in the chart. There are an odd number of warp ends, each one represented by a square on the chart. Read the chart from left to the centre then back to the right. See p. 30 for winding a striped warp. Each time there is a colour change on the chart, knot the new thread to the previous one at a warping post. The weft is the same colour as the warp selvedges and the braid is woven completely in plain weave.

There are many variations on this idea so try designing some of your own. Remember each complete turn around the warping posts gives two warp ends. A stripe must be at least two warp ends and multiples of two will give broader stripes. Alternating single coloured warp ends by tying threads together at each post will give a horizontally striped pattern.

Striped backstrap braid, woven in a smooth mercerised cotton with the pattern chart above. Woven by the author.

Brocaded backstrap braid

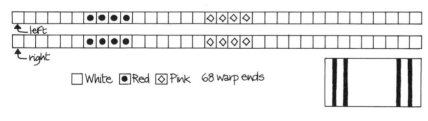

☐ White ● Red ◇ Pink   68 warp ends

This braid is an introduction to brocading using a medium thickness natural cotton for the warp and ground weft, and thicker stranded cotton for the pattern wefts (see photos on p. 34 and facing p. 32). As you become more skilful you could try using finer threads, but bear in mind that the warp for backstrap weaving must be very strong and smooth, so it won't break or stick to the heddles.

The chart shows the warping pattern for the ground weave, which is warp-faced with a striped border. The designs for brocading can be worked out on squared paper. There are many ideas which can be adapted from folk embroidery, or you could look in books and museums for examples of traditional textile designs and motifs. I have included only a few ideas here (Diag. 38).

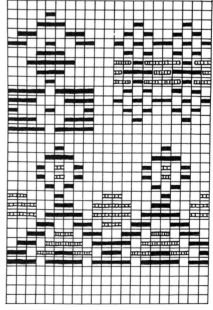

Diagram 38

Tablet weaving

Egyptian tablet woven braid, 7th–10th century AD. Courtesy of the Victoria and Albert Museum, London.

Introduction

Tablet or card weaving is an ingenious way of making braids to create strikingly beautiful patterns. It requires little equipment yet can produce more sophisticated designs than any other textile technique. The warp is threaded through holes in the tablets, then either stretched in tension between two fixed points, or attached by the far end to a door-handle or clamps fixed to a table and by the other end to the waist of the weaver. The unique feature of tablet weaving is the infinite variety of patterns which can be created by the order in which the warp is threaded through the tablets and the way the tablets are turned.

Tablet weaving has a warp-faced weave structure, where only the warp is visible in the finished braid, while the weft holds the warp together and remains hidden in the weaving. The weave structure in tablet weaving has a particular characteristic unlike any other textile. As each tablet is turned the warp threads through its holes twist in a spiral (Diag. 40 opposite). With a four-holed square tablet this produces a four-ply rope. If several tablets are turned together and a weft is passed through the shed between each turn, all the twisted ropes are held together (Diag. 40). If the tablets are turned towards the weaver the warp threads spiral in one direction, and if they are turned away the opposite spiral is made. It is the combination of different coloured threads which are brought to the top at each turn of the tablets, and the changing angle of the twist, depending on which way the tablets turn, which creates the vivid and intricate patterns.

The earliest tablet woven braids date back to Ancient Egypt; the technique was later used in Ancient Rome and spread to Northern Europe. Early braids and wooden and bone tablets have been found dating from the Iron Age in Denmark and Scandinavia. Later, tablet weaving techniques became highly developed in Europe in the Middle Ages, with the use of silk, gold and silver threads. Braids were woven to decorate church vestments and court costume, and as commemorative bands depicting special events using woven letters to convey dates and messages.

Tablet woven braids have also been highly developed in Asia and they are still made today in Nepal, Northern India, and China, and in North Africa. Tablet weavers can be seen today in Morocco, weaving woollen braids to decorate the traditional djellabahs worn as everyday clothing.

Preparation and materials

The tablets

You can buy tablets from weaving suppliers or make your own from stiff card. Tablets can be square, triangular or hexagonal but the square tablet is easiest to work with and gives very good results. All the braids in this section are made with square tablets. To make your own, you will need some stiff card, a hole-puncher, and a sharp paper-cutting knife. Mark and cut squares of card 6 cm ($2\frac{3}{8}$ in) in size and round off the corners so the warp threads won't catch on them. Punch a hole in each corner and label each hole A, B, C and D clockwise (Diag. 39). This lettered side is the right side or front of the tablet. Cut a square hole in the centre as well so you can tie the tablets together when you stop weaving. Colour the corresponding edges with coloured pens so that when you are weaving you will easily see if one tablet is out of order. The number of tablets you need depends on the width of the braid you want to weave; the wider the braid the more tablets it takes. A set of 30 would be ample to begin with.

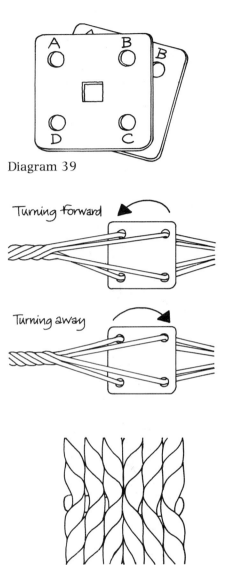

Diagram 39

Turning forward

Turning away

The warp

Tablet weaving has a warp-faced weave so only the warp threads show on the surface of the braid. Like backstrap weaving, the warp is stretched in firm tension whilst you are weaving, but as the tablets are both supported by the warp threads and constantly rubbing against them it is essential you choose very strong smooth yarns, without elasticity. As a beginner, you could start with 2-ply rug yarn or woollen worsted, (see p. 28) or corded or mercerised cotton. Avoid fuzzy, loopy or textured threads and if you want to use hand-spun wool, it needs to be tightly and evenly spun. If you want to re-spin yarn you have purchased, to make it stronger, see p. 18. As you become more experienced you may want to try linen or silk, which give a rich and luxurious finish to braids.

Diagram 40

The weft

The weft doesn't show on the surface of the weaving, except sometimes at the centre of the braid when you change the turning sequence in some patterns. The edges of the braid will look much neater if you use a weft which is the same colour as the warp threaded through the first and last tablet. Wind the weft in a butterfly (Diag. 68, p. 59), or around a thin tube of paper (Diag 2, p. 12).

Other equipment

The tablets are the major part of your equipment, but here are a few extras which will help in the weaving:

> Two pieces of wooden baton for the front and back sticks, $7 \times 1 \times \frac{1}{4}$ in, $(18 \times 2 \times 1.25 \, \text{cm})$.
> One piece of baton for the beater, $7 \times \frac{3}{4} \times 8$ in $(18 \times 2 \times 0.75 \, \text{cm})$. These sticks should be longer if you want to weave braids wider than 7.5 cm (3 in).
> A pair of G clamps, a leather belt, strong cord, scissors, a tape measure and knitting needle, coloured pens and squared paper.

The front and back sticks act in the same way as the warp beams on a backstrap loom. These aren't essential as you can simply tie your warp ends in an overhand knot at each end and loop tying cords through the knots (Diag. 48, p. 43). However, I find that attaching the warp in the correct threading order to the back stick helps when you thread the tablets (Diag. 43) and tying the warp with weaver's knots to the front stick (Diag. 48) keeps the threads even and flat at the beginning, so that when you begin your braid it gets off to a straight start.

The pattern chart

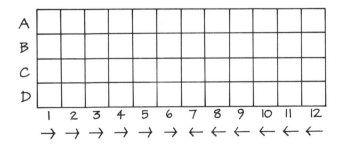

Thread the yarn from the back to the front of each tablet

Thread the yarn from the front to the back of each tablet

Diagram 41

The pattern chart is a grid of squares in which the patterns for tablet weaving can be designed. As we are concentrating on square four-holed tablets in this book, all the charts are four squares in depth to represent the holes in each tablet. At the left of the chart the letters A, B, C and D correspond with the holes in each tablet. Along the bottom edge the squares are numbered to represent each tablet. In this example the braid will be woven with 12 tablets. The arrows along the bottom edge tell you in which direction to thread the yarn through the holes in each tablet. Threading is either from back to front or front to back (see Diags. 41 and 44).

There are two basic approaches to designing patterns for tablet weaving, and they differ both in the design on the chart and the sequence of turning the tablets in the weaving.

Method 1

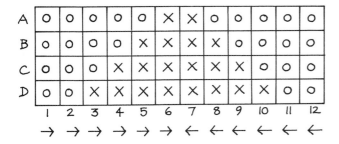

This chart outlines the design for the weave by making a pattern with symbols in the squares of the chart. Each symbol represents a different coloured thread, and according to its position on the chart will tell you which coloured thread to put through the relevant hole in each tablet and in which direction.

The design on this chart is of half a diamond on a contrasting background. Each horizontal row of squares will be the equivalent to one row of weaving, so the chart represents four rows which make up one half of the diamond pattern. To get an idea of how the pattern will repeat along the length of the braid, put a mirror to the bottom edge of the chart. You will see the pattern is inverted to make a complete diamond. This comes about by turning the tablets four quarter-turns towards you, then four quarter-turns away from you. The weft is inserted in each row, between the turns of the tablets, to hold the twist in the warp threads at each turn.

Read pages 41 to 44, then set up and weave this diamond design first so you understand how the chart relates to the weave. You could then follow it up with Braids 1 and 2 on p. 47. These first braids will give you a sound basis from which you can design patterns yourself, using the alternating turning sequence.

Method 2

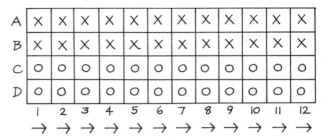

This method of tablet weaving uses a much simpler pattern chart but a more complex turning sequence. Try weaving braids according to method 1 first before you attempt method 2, so you have thoroughly mastered the basic turning sequence.

The pattern chart above shows that all the A and B holes are threaded with one colour, and the C and D holes with a contrasting colour. The scope for design possibilities in this method lies not in the repeated turning of the tablets forward and back as in method 1, but in varying the turning sequences and positions of individual tablets.

Threading the tablets in this way results in a warp with one colour on top and the other below. By turning individual tablets in different directions, the colours will change position, that is, they will move from on top of the braid to underneath, and vice versa. As a result, the patterns are reversible and so this weave is sometimes described as double-face weaving.

Setting up tablet weaving

Preparing the warp

Once you have decided which pattern to weave, and have drawn a pattern chart using methods 1 or 2, you then need to prepare the warp.

First of all you need to decide the length of braid you want to weave, then cut the threads one and a half times the finished length including an allowance of about 7.5 cm (3 in) each end for fringes. Refer to the chart to see how many threads of each colour you will need. Let's use the chart for method 1 on p. 39. Count each group of symbols; in this example there are 28 threads in colour 0, and 20 threads in colour X. If you want to weave a braid 2 metres (2 yds) long, you will need: 28 threads in 0, and 20 threads in X, each 3 metres (3¼ yds) long.

There are several ways of cutting the warp for tablet weaving. If you are making a short narrow braid, you will be able to wind off each length individually from balls of yarn. Measure your threads carefully, cut them and lay them over the back of a chair where you can pick them up easily when threading the tablets.

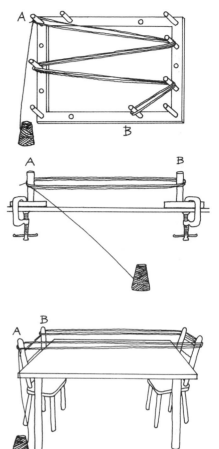

However, for longer braids it is much more accurate to wind the warp around two fixed objects. You can use a warping board, warping posts clamped to a table (see how to make posts on p. 29), or simply wind the warp around two chairs (Diag. 42). Whatever you use, set the two fixed points A and B the required distance apart for your warp length. Wind each colour group around points A and B until you have the number you need. Remember each complete turn gives two warp ends. Cut the threads at each point for Method 1 patterns and put them to one side. For Method 2 patterns, which always need coloured threads in pairs, cut the threads at one point only. In both cases place the threads carefully across a table, keeping each colour group separate.

The simplest way to tie the warp, prior to threading it through the tablets, is to knot all the threads together in an overhand knot at one end, lay them flat on the table, and weight the far end down with books. However, I find a neater way is to attach the warp to a flat stick, in the same order as the chart. Starting on the left, take the eight threads which correspond to the symbols on the chart for tablets 1 and 2, knot them together and tie them to the stick with a lark's head knot (Diag. 43). Continue with each group in turn until all the threads are tied to the stick.

Diagram 42

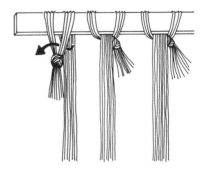

Diagram 43

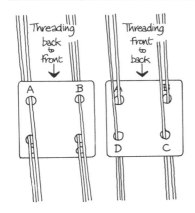

Diagram 44

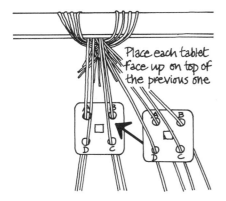

Diagram 45

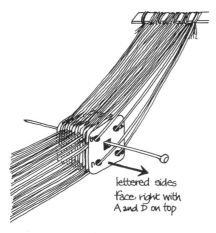

Diagram 46

Threading the tablets

Weight the stick with the warp attached down on the table by putting a pile of books on one end. Put your pattern chart where you can see it easily and have your tablets near at hand. Starting on the left of the threads, pick up the first four threads which correspond with the first column of symbols on the chart for tablet 1. Check the arrows on the chart so you know in which direction to put the threads through the holes, (Diags. 41 and 44). Take the coloured thread for symbol A and put it through hole A in the tablet. Repeat with the other three through holes B, C and D. Put the tablet *face up* on the table. Now pick up the next four threads and thread them according to the symbols on the chart through holes A, B, C and D in the second tablet (Diag. 45). Place the second tablet *face up on top* of the previous one. Continue until you have completed them all. Pick up the whole pack of tablets and turn them on end, so the lettered side is facing to your right with holes A and D uppermost. Thread a cord through the centre holes and tie the tablets together to keep them securely in position, or alternatively push a long knitting needle through them (Diag. 46) and loop an elastic band onto the needle and across the top of the pack.

Tensioning the warp

Put the stick holding the warp on the edge of the table and clamp it down tightly. If your warp is very long and it is going to be difficult to stretch it out in full in the space you have, rotate some of the warp around the stick before clamping it down. You can unroll it as the weaving progresses.

Pick up the tablets, loosen the cord a little or take the elastic band off, and start easing the tablets down the warp towards you pulling fairly firmly but with care. The tablets must not turn but stay in their original position. The threads may get a little tangled so use your fingers to comb them out, especially just in front of the tablets. Separate each tablet in turn and check that the threads aren't twisted. If you have threaded the tablets onto a knitting needle it makes sliding the tablets down the warp easier. When the tablets are about 30 cm (12 in) from the front end of the warp, pull all the threads together and trim them so they are all exactly the same length (Diag. 47).

Put the tablets down and get everything ready to start weaving. You will need a chair if you want to sit down to weave, and next to it a ball of weft, a batten or ruler for beating the weft, a bulldog clip and the chart. I also find it useful to make a little card guide with the turning directions marked on either side. Turn this around when your turning sequence changes. If you get distracted this helps you to know where you are in the weaving.

Now tie a belt around your waist and attach the warp to it in either of the following ways. Tie an overhand knot in the warp, loop a cord through it and tie the cord to your belt, or alternatively you can tie the warp to a front stick (Diag. 48). First tie the stick to your belt with two cords, leaving a gap in between of about 10 cm (4 in). Take hold of the outer eight threads on the left of the warp and tie them with a weaver's knot over the stick. (Diag. 48) Take the outer eight threads on the right and tie them to the stick. It may seem at this stage that you need two pairs of hands to do all this, so help yourself by resting the tablets on a stool while you tie the ends. The tablets can't get out of order while you still have the cord or needle through the centre. Now take groups of threads in the centre and tie them. Try to keep the threads straight between the tablets and the stick. Check that the tension of all the threads is even by sitting upright and pressing your hand against the warp. If it isn't, adjust the knots where necessary. Remember that it is how you sit that will create the tension in the warp, so always sit upright. This can be good exercise for you too! Now push all the threads closely together and you are ready to weave (Diag. 49).

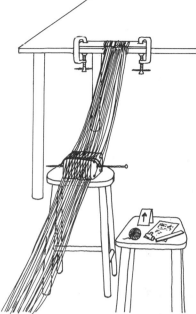

Diagram 47

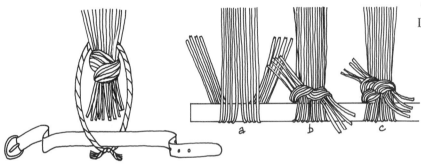

Diagram 48

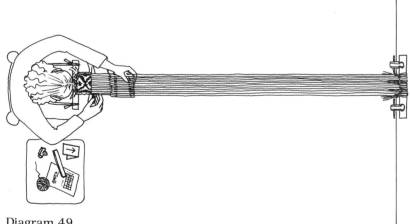

Diagram 49

Turning the tablets forward
start

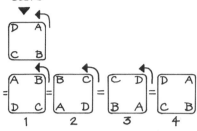

Turning the tablets away
start

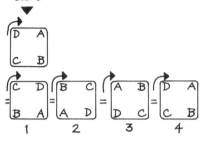

Diagram 50

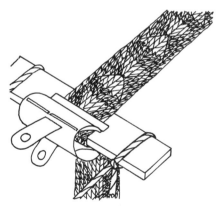

Diagram 51

Weaving

Make sure all the tablets are correctly in position, and untie the cord or remove the needle through the centre of the tablets.

Turning the tablets four quarter turns each way
This is the basic weaving technique for the simplest braid,

1 Starting with holes A and D uppermost, pass the weft through the existing open shed from right to left and beat it towards you. Leave an end of about 10 cm (4 in).
2 Turn all the tablets one quarter turn towards you so holes A and B are on top. At first you may be able to turn only one tablet at a time, but after some practice you should be able to grasp half the tablets in each hand and turn the whole pack. Ease them along the warp a little to help separate the threads.
3 Put the batten between the upper and lower threads in front of the tablets and ease the open shed towards you. Check for any stray threads, pass the weft back through this shed leaving a small loop on the left edge.
4 Turn the tablets towards you so B and C are on top. Open this shed, and pull the weft in from the last row and beat. This will help to maintain an even width along the braid. Insert the weft into this shed from right to left.
5 Turn the tablets towards you so C and D are on top. Pull the weft loop in from the last row, beat, and insert the weft into this shed from left to right.
6 Turn the tablets again, so A and D are on top. Pull the loop, beat and insert the weft in this shed from right to left.

You now reverse the turning sequence, by turning the tablets four quarters away from you, so the uppermost holes will be C and D, B and C, A and B, then A and D again. After a few pattern repeats, you will be able to see how the woven pattern relates to the turning direction. When it becomes difficult to reach the weaving, secure the tablets again, untie the knots at the front stick and slip the weaving over the stick and clamp it with a bulldog clip (Diag. 51).

Turning the tablets in one direction

Different patterns can be made by turning all the tablets continuously in one direction only. This can cause two problems, though. Firstly, the warp behind the tablets becomes completely twisted in one direction so that eventually you can't move the tablets up the warp. You will therefore need to untie the warp at the back, untwist the threads, and re-tie them. Swivel hooks holding the warp at the back can help with this problem. Secondly, the braid itself becomes slightly distorted at the edges because of the continuous twist. To alleviate this, turn the outer two tablets in the *opposite* direction to the main pack. If the pattern extends to the edges this could spoil it, so add a border in a contrasting colour when you are threading up. This will set off the centre pattern well and the opposite turning sequence won't show (see photo facing p. 33, no. 5 Braid 4).

After you have turned the tablets, use the side of your hand to open the shed between the upper and lower threads, bringing it towards you.

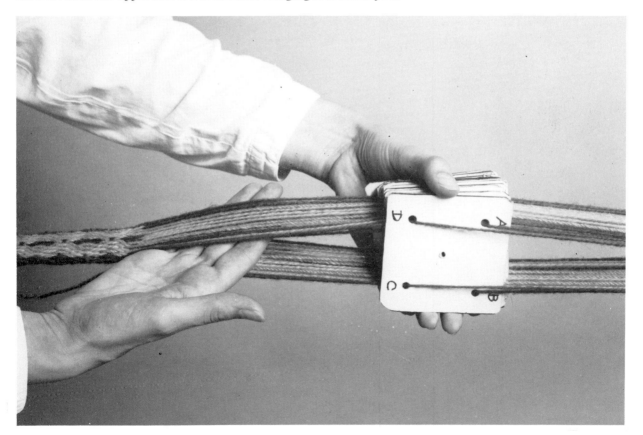

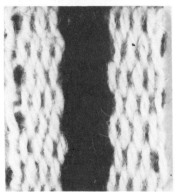

Variations in the positions and turning of the tablets

Here are some variations you can try. They are all based on the basic pattern chart for Method 2. Before you start to weave, turn all the tablets so holes A and B are uppermost.

1 For a plain reversible braid, turn one quarter turn towards so B and C are on top, turn away to A and B on top, then away again to A and D on top, towards to A and B, and towards again to B and C. Repeat by turning away twice, then towards twice. See photo, top.

2 For a reversible striped braid, take a centre group of tablets, say 4 if you have 12 in all, and turn them two quarter turns away before you begin to weave. Then turn all the tablets away twice and towards twice and repeat (see second photo).

3 Flip the tablets so the colours are arranged as in chart **a**. Turn all the tablets four quarter turns towards, then four turns away, to give the zig-zag pattern in third photo.

top holes ▶	X	O	O	X	X	O	O	X	X	O	O	X
	X	X	O	O	X	X	O	O	X	X	O	O
bottom holes ▶	O	X	X	O	O	X	X	O	O	X	X	O
	O	O	X	X	O	O	X	X	O	O	X	X
	1	2	3	4	5	6	7	8	9	10	11	12

a

4 Flip the tablets according to chart **b**, and turn four quarter turns towards, then four away for a diagonal pattern. (see bottom photo).

top holes ▶	X	X	O	O	X	X	O	O	X	X	O	O
	X	X	O	O	X	X	O	O	X	X	O	O
bottom holes ▶	O	O	X	X	O	O	X	X	O	O	X	X
	O	O	X	X	O	O	X	X	O	O	X	X
	1	2	3	4	5	6	7	8	9	10	11	12

b

Various patterns made from the basic chart for Method 2. Top to bottom:
1 Plain reversible braid   2 Striped reversible braid   3 Zig-zag pattern
4 Diagonal pattern. Woven by the author.

Braid 1

	1	2	3	4	5	6	7	8	9	10	11	12	13	14	15	16
A	O	O	O	●	●	X	X	●	●	●	X	X	●	●	O	O
B	O	O	●	●	X	X	●	●	●	●	X	X	●	●	O	O
C	O	●	●	X	X	●	●	O	O	●	●	X	X	●	●	O
D	O	●	X	X	●	●	O	O	O	O	●	●	X	X	●	O

→ → → → → → → → ← ← ← ← ← ← ← ←

Method 1
4 colours

This braid is suitable for beginners. Thread the tablets according to the chart and set up the warp (see p. 41). The pattern shown in photo, top, is made by turning the tablets four quarter turns towards and then four turns away alternately.

Braid 2

	1	2	3	4	5	6	7	8	9	10	11	12
A	●	X	□	□	O	X	X	X	●	●	●	●
B	●	●	X	□	□	O	X	X	X	●	●	●
C	●	●	●	X	□	□	O	X	X	X	●	●
D	●	●	●	●	X	□	□	O	X	X	X	●

← ← ← ← ← ← ← ← ← ← ← ←

Method 1
4 colours

This braid is suitable for beginners. Thread the tablets according to the chart and set up the warp (see p. 41). This pattern is also based on four quarter turns towards and four turns away (see photo, bottom).

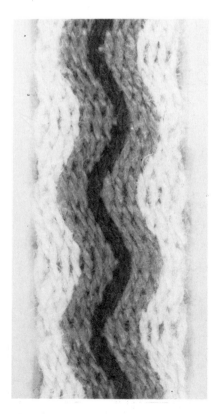

Top: Braid 1
Bottom: Braid 2

Braid 3

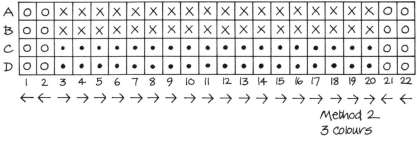

	1	2	3	4	5	6	7	8	9	10	11	12
A	●	●	●	●	●	●	●	●	●	●	●	●
B	●	●	●	X	X	□	□	X	X	●	●	●
C	●	●	X	X	□	□	□	□	X	X	●	●
D	●	X	X	□	○	○	○	○	□	X	X	●

→ → → → → → ← ← ← ← ← ←

Method 1
4 colours

In this braid you can try varying the position and turning of the tablets. Thread the tablets according to the chart, and set up the warp (see p. 41). Vary the basic turning sequence by turning the tablets 8, 12 or 16 turns towards and then away, and see how the pattern changes. Shift the positions of the tablets in the pack, and try various turning sequences (see photo on left).

Braid 4

	1	2	3	4	5	6	7	8	9	10	11	12	13	14	15	16	17	18	19	20	21	22
A	○	○	X	X	X	X	X	X	X	X	X	X	X	X	X	X	X	X	X	X	○	○
B	○	○	X	X	X	X	X	X	X	X	X	X	X	X	X	X	X	X	X	X	○	○
C	○	○	●	●	●	●	●	●	●	●	●	●	●	●	●	●	●	●	●	●	○	○
D	○	○	●	●	●	●	●	●	●	●	●	●	●	●	●	●	●	●	●	●	○	○

← ← → → → → → → → → → → → → → → → → → → ← ←

Method 2
3 colours

Try Braids 1 and 2 before attempting this pattern. Thread the tablets according to the chart, threading 1 first and placing the rest on top, one by one, until 22 is uppermost. Tip the whole pack so A and D are on top, facing right. Turn each tablet so the letters in the top far left corner read A, B, C, D etc. Number all the tablets below the top left hole 1 to 22, from left to right, to help you keep them in order while you are weaving. Set up the warp so you are ready to weave (p. 41).

For the diagonal pattern shown in the photo, begin by sliding tablets 1 to 4 up the warp away from you, to separate them from the main pack. Turn tablets 1 to 4 towards you, the rest away, insert the weft and beat. Repeat once more. Take another two tablets from the main pack and slide them up alongside 1 to 4. Turn tablets 1 to 6 towards you, the rest away, insert the weft and beat. Repeat. Continue in this way until tablets 1 to 22 are together and turn them all towards you, insert the weft and beat. Repeat.

To reverse the pattern follow the same steps but begin on the right with tablets 19 to 22 turning towards, and the rest away. Continue until tablets 1 to 22 are together again.

Top: Braid 3
Bottom: Braid 4
Woven by the author.

Braid 5

Refer to the chart for Braid 4 and thread up the tablets in the same way, so A and D are on top, facing right. Turn all the tablets so A and B are uppermost, thus bringing one colour to the top of the warp and the other below. You are now in step 1 of the basic turning sequence.

The basic turning sequence is:

1 Turn all the tablets towards you, so A and B are on top.
2 Turn all the tablets away from you, so B and C are on top.
3 Turn all the tablets towards you, so A and B are on top.
4 Turn all the tablets away from you, so A and D are on top.

This will give a plain braid with one colour above and the other below. To make letters or motifs, you will need to separate groups of tablets and turn them in the opposite direction, so the lower colour comes to the top and makes a contrasting motif and vice versa below.

For the *background* colour, slide the tablets up the warp away from you and turn them in the *basic turning sequence*. For coloured *letters*, *patterns* or *borders*, slide the appropriate tablets down the warp towards you and turn them the *opposite way to the basic turning sequence*. In any one row of the weaving, therefore, background tablets are being turned in the basic turning sequence while pattern tablets are being turned in the opposite direction.

The plan in Diag. 52 shows how you can design letters and motifs on squared paper. The vertical lines represent the number of tablets and the horizontal lines equal four turns of the tablets. Draw thicker, coloured vertical lines to make the shapes of the design, so you can see in each of the horizontal bands which tablets are pattern tablets and which are background. Re-arrange the tablets after every four turns to continue the pattern. Always keep the pattern tablets separated and nearer to you while the background tablets are further up the warp away from you (see photo facing p. 33).

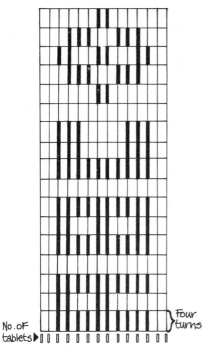

No. of tablets ▶

Four turns

Background = basic turning sequence
Letters = opposite turning sequence

Diagram 52

Finishing braids

Finishing off a braid is the last, and very important, step in the weaving. I have included a few suggestions here for finishing individual braids, but you can of course join any number of narrow braids together to make larger items and there are some ideas on p. 108. Look at the photo facing p. 96 too. Sew braids together in the same way as joining slits in tapestry (see p. 63), Diag. 77.

Darning in wefts
Darn in any ends of wefts horizontally across the weave in warp-faced braids, and vertically in weft-faced braids, for about 3 cm ($1\frac{1}{4}$ in). Try to match the colours in the weave.

Mending broken warp ends
Untie the warp ends you knotted together, and darn one up and one down the weave so they are parallel with the warp for about 5 cm (2 in), then trim.

Twisted or plied fringes
Take a single thread and twist it tightly in one direction. Do this with several threads then twist them together in the opposite direction and trim neatly (Diag. 53).

Plaited fringes
Make plaits with three single or grouped threads for a three-strand plait or make a four-strand plait or cord (Diag. 53).

Knotted fringes

A macramé square knot needs four single or grouped threads. For a second row, make the knots on alternate pairs (Diag. 53). A macramé fringe takes up about one and a half times the finished length of the threads, so leave long threads if you want this kind of fringe.

Wrapping

I have described wrapping on p. 83. Pick out certain colours in the braid and wrap groups of threads in those colours for a bold edging, or combine the wrapping with beads and knots.

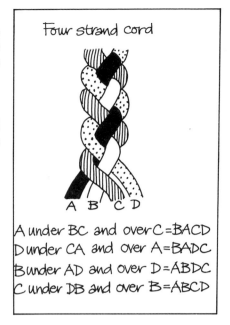

Four strand cord

A under BC and over C = BACD
D under CA and over A = BADC
B under AD and over D = ABDC
C under DB and over B = ABCD

Diagram 53

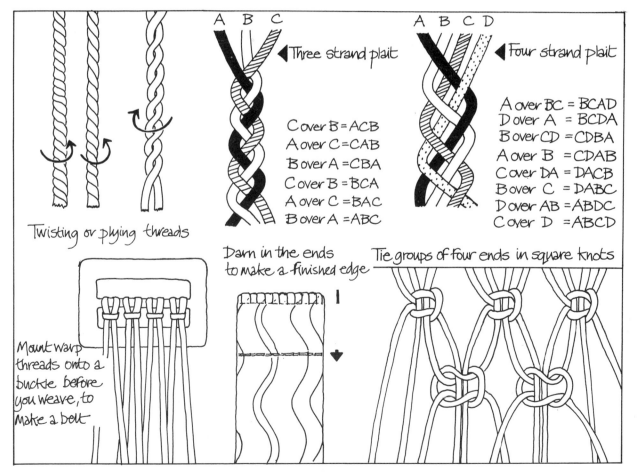

Three strand plait

C over B = ACB
A over C = CAB
B over A = CBA
C over B = BCA
A over C = BAC
B over A = ABC

Four strand plait

A over BC = BCAD
D over A = BCDA
B over CD = CDBA
A over B = CDAB
C over DA = DACB
B over C = DABC
D over AB = ABDC
C over D = ABCD

Twisting or plying threads

Mount warp threads onto a buckle before you weave, to make a belt

Darn in the ends to make a finished edge

Tie groups of four ends in square knots

Tapestry weaving

Introduction

Tapestry weaving is a type of weaving which produces heavy textiles with boldly patterned or pictorial images. The woollen weft is woven through a highly tensioned warp and beaten down so the surface of the weave is entirely weft-faced. The combination of the weave structure and the colours and designs created by the weft gives tapestry its sumptuous quality.

Fragments of tapestries have been found in the Ancient Egyptian tombs, and in the burial grounds of Ancient Peru, and the brilliant use of techniques and expressive interpretation of mythological themes show that in both these early cultures tapestry weaving was already highly developed. By the Middle Ages tapestry weaving had spread to Europe, probably brought by the Arab weavers who had inherited their skills from the Copts in Egypt. They took the craft to Spain and from there it spread to France, Germany, Scandinavia and England. The early mediaeval tapestries are amongst the finest, full of life and originality, because the weavers were free to make their own interpretations of the designs prepared by the artist, and could use their skills to the utmost. In Paris and Flanders, the centres of tapestry at this time, superb hangings were woven depicting important events, court scenes and popular legends.

By the early seventeenth century, though, tapestries had become no more than ornate woven copies of oil paintings. The weavers were expected to follow the artist's design slavishly, using hundreds of differently coloured yarns to make the woven replicas complete, so that all the spontaneity and technical innovation of the earlier tapestries was destroyed.

It wasn't until the late nineteenth century and the growth of the Arts and Crafts movement that a revival was brought about, principally by William Morris. Later, in France in the 1920s, the artist Jean Lurçat foresaw that tapestry would become a highly creative medium for both the contemporary artist and craftsperson to work in. Now, modern tapestry weavers, like their mediaeval predecessors, can create and freely interpret their designs and experiment with colours, techniques, and ideas.

An early upright loom, used for rug weaving, (reproduced from *Studies in Primitive Looms*, by H. Ling Roth, by courtesy of Bankfield Museum, Halifax).

Preparation and materials

The warp

The warp for tapestry must be very strong, as it is held in considerable tension on the frame, and smooth so the weft can be packed down easily. Tightly spun cotton twine is the best type of warp as it will not rub or fray. The colour is unimportant, as the warp doesn't show, so use a natural undyed cotton.

The weft

Woollen yarns are mostly used for tapestry as they cover the warp well. Different types of wool can give a variety of effects. 2-ply rug yarn, good for a beginner to use, has a thick, slightly coarse texture, soft-spun stranded tapestry is finer, and worsted gives a smoother, firm finish. The latter, if it is very fine, can be stranded together four or five times. Fancy threads such as silks, metallic or textured threads can be used to give interest. See p. 10 for more about yarns.

Other equipment

You will also need: a fork, or a comb with a handle for a beater, scissors, a large-eyed, blunt carpet needle. For small frames: a flat stick 2 cm × 3 mm ($\frac{3}{4}$ in × $\frac{1}{8}$ in) for a shed stick, one or two round sticks 1.25 cm ($\frac{1}{2}$ in) thick for heddle sticks. For large frames: two round sticks 2.5 cm (1 in) thick for leash bars. All sticks should equal the width of the frame. A black permanent pen and white paper for a cartoon.

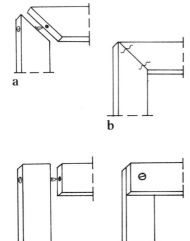

a

b

c   d

Diagram 54 – see text overleaf

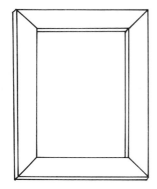

Diagram 55

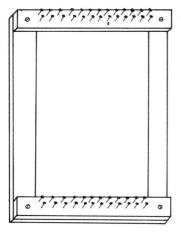

Diagram 56

Diagram 57

How to make a frame

A simple frame
A sturdy frame is all that is required to weave a tapestry. Making your own is satisfying and cost-effective. The inside length should be at least 10 cm (4 in) longer than the finished tapestry and the inside width an additional 5 cm (2 in). A frame measuring 38 × 50 cm (15 × 20 in), using wooden baton 3 × 1.25 cm (1¼ × ½ in) would be a good size to start with. A larger frame, 122 × 183 cm (4 × 6 ft), using thicker wood 5 × 2 cm (2 × 1 in), would give ample scope for more ambitious projects.

Diag. 54 shows different ways of making joints for frames. Diags. 54a, b and c are for flat frames, and Diag. 54d shows how the top and bottom pieces rest on the sides. The important thing is to make sure the joints are strong and secure, using wood glue as well as screws, and the wood is sanded smooth at the outer top and bottom edges. The simple frame in Diag. 55, has the warp wound continuously around it from top to bottom in a figure of eight. To space the warp evenly, make pencil marks along the top and bottom of the frame according to the warp spacing you want. See also pp. 55 and 87 on warp spacing. Here is a guide for the three most commonly used spacings.

Make marks 1.25 cm (½ in) apart for a warp spacing of four ends per 2.5 cm (1 in), and marks 1 cm (⅜ in) apart for a spacing of six ends per 2.5 cm (1 in). For eight ends per 2.5 cm (1 in) the marks should be 6 mm (¼ in) apart.

A frame with nails
An alternative to the simple frame is to put nails in the top and bottom of the frame, for the warp to be wrapped around, Diag. 56. This is the easiest way to warp a frame. Use rust-proof nails 2.5 cm (1 in) long and stagger the nails by spacing them in two rows so the wood won't split. Mark and position the nails as follows. Draw two lines 1.25 cm (½ in) apart along both the top and bottom pieces of the frame. For a warp spacing of four warp ends per 2.5 cm (1 in), make marks 2.5 cm (1 in) apart along the top lines starting from the inside edge of the frame on the left. Then do the same on the lower lines, but start 1.25 cm (½ in) further along so the nails are staggered in two rows. It is very important to make the marks line up on the top and bottom of the frame so your warp will be straight and at right angles to the sides. For a warp spacing of six warp ends per 2.5 cm (1 in) make marks 2 cm (¾ in) apart, and for eight ends per 2.5 cm (1 in) make marks 1.25 cm (½ in) apart. See also pp. 55 and 87 on warp spacing. Hammer the nails into the wood at the marks, making sure they will be firm enough to support the warp. You can add hinges to the frame as shown in Diag. 57. These can be held in place with two bolts and wing nuts through the sides of the frame, and make weaving much easier as the frame can stand up on the table.

A large tapestry frame

Large frames can be purchased from weaving equipment suppliers but can be very expensive. Like the smaller frames they can be made for a fraction of the cost. If you are a beginner to weaving it is probably wiser to work on a smaller frame first, to get the feel of tapestry and what you want to do. When you are ready to attempt a bigger project you will then have a clearer idea of what you want.

The frame in Diag. 58 is one which I like and works well. The warp is wound around the top (a) and bottom (b) beams. The top beam is held within the frame with long bolts and nuts, so you can tighten or loosen the warp. The leash bar (c) is held to the front of the frame with G-clamps, for leashes to be attached to it. Another similar round bar is put through the warp in the opposite shed, Diags. 67 and on p.14. The feet are optional, as you could prop the frame against the wall, but a solid free-standing frame means you can pull more firmly on the leashes to open the sheds. Like the simple frame you can make marks for warp spacing along the beams, or alternatively cut grooves in the beams to hold the warp ends. If you do this, think which warp spacings will give you most flexibility. A good all-round spacing would be grooves every 6 mm ($\frac{1}{4}$ in) enabling you to weave at eight ends per 2.5 cm (1 in) for a fine weave, and by winding on alternate grooves you could make a thicker weave at four ends per 2.5 cm (1 in).

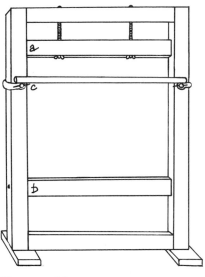

Diagram 58

Warping the frame

Warp spacing

The spacing of the warp relates to the intricacy of the design, so the closer and finer the warp, the more detail you can weave. Spacing the warp at four, six or eight ends per 2.5 cm (1 in) will give you a lot of flexibility. At four ends you will have a medium thick weave, good for rugs, cushions, and boldly patterned items. At eight, you can get quite a lot of detail into pictorial tapestry. If you are uncertain about the thickness of your warp, try samples first by winding a narrow warp around a book, trying each of the above spacings in turn. Weave different thicknesses of weft through the warp with a needle. The weft should cover the warp easily, without causing the warp to bunch up or bulge at the edges. On the whole, remember that the more warp there is to the centimetre (or inch), whether because of its thickness or number of ends, then the finer the weft must be. Double warping on a frame can enable you to weave more detail in some parts of the tapestry. See p. 87.

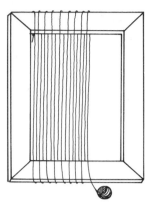

Diagram 59

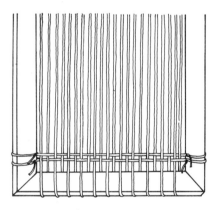

Diagram 60

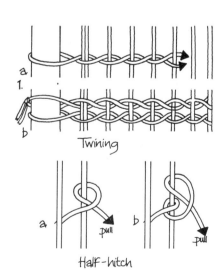

Twining

Half-hitch

Diagram 61

Warping a simple frame

Decide on your warp spacing and make marks the correct distance apart on the top and bottom of the frame (see p. 54). Measure off the amount of warp you will need for the full width, allowing a little extra. Tie one end to the first mark on the top left of the frame. Take the warp down to the corresponding mark at the bottom, over and behind the wood and back up and over the wood at the top on the second mark. Continue winding in a figure of eight, keeping the tension even and fairly firm across the warp, and tie the end at the last mark (Diag. 59 and Diag. 4 on p. 13).

The heading

You now need to space the warp ends evenly by drawing them together from behind and in front of the wood of the frame. Take a length of warp and tie it to the left side of the frame. Pass it over and under each warp end, except at each side where two ends are doubled together to help strengthen the edges of the weaving. Hold the thread in an arc, pull it tightly and beat it down until it is parallel with the bottom of the frame. Tie it to the right of the frame. Repeat once more in the other shed (Diag. 60). These threads are removed when the warp is cut from the frame. If you want a fringe allowance, insert a strip of card through the warp first, and put the heading in just above it.

The selvedge

This is an edging at the beginning and the end of the tapestry to secure the weaving. There are three alternative ways of doing this.

Twining

Cut a length of warp thread about six times the width of the frame. Take the centre of the thread and loop it around the left side of the frame. Twist the two ends in a figure of eight around each warp end, pulling firmly as you go, and continue across the warp (Diag. 61). Turn around on the right side of the frame and make a second row, twisting in the opposite direction. Suitable for a fringed edging. See also p. 77.

The half-hitch

Cut a length of warp thread about six times the width of the frame. Starting on the left take the thread over and around one warp end. Repeat on the same warp end and pull the hitch tight (Diag. 61). Continue across the warp. Suitable for a fringed edging.

The turn-back

Weave about 2.5 cm (1 in) of plain weft-faced weave in the warp thread. Then make a row of half-hitches in warp thread or the first colour of weft in your tapestry. Suitable for turning back a hem on the edges of a tapestry.

Warping a frame with nails

Decide on your warp spacing and mark and hammer in nails on the top and bottom of the frame (see p. 54). Tie the warp to the first nail at the top left. Take the warp down to the corresponding nail at the bottom, round it from left to right and back up to the top nail again, round it from right to left and down again to the same first nail. This makes three warp ends together, two of which will be doubled together at the edge.

Now take the warp across to the next nail at the bottom of the frame, up on the right-hand side of it to the corresponding top nail and around and down on the left-hand side. Continue in this way, winding up on the right and down on the left side of each pair of corresponding nails. (Diags. 62, 63 and Diag. 3 on p. 13). Always maintain a fairly tight and even tension throughout. Finish with three turns on the last two nails and tie securely. Now insert a strip of card about 5 cm (2 in) deep in the bottom of the warp. Omit the heading and make a selvedge (see p. 56).

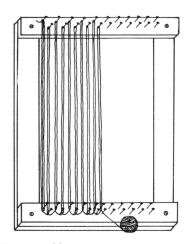

Diagram 62

Warping a large frame

The warp is wound around the top and bottom beams continuously. Remove the leash bar and wind the warp as you would for a simple frame, by winding in a figure of eight over the marks or grooves on the top and bottom beams (see p.55 and Diag. 64). Keep the tension firm. You can of course slacken off or tighten the warp on this frame with the tension bolts. Follow instructions on p. 56 for the heading and choice of selvedge. For larger tapestries, which need to be backed, I suggest you have a turn-back and bottom.

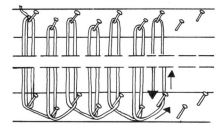

Diagram 63

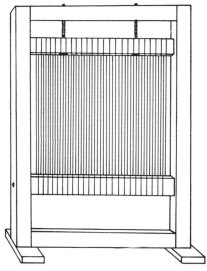

Diagram 64

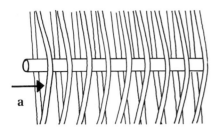

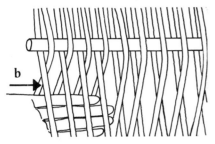

Diagram 65

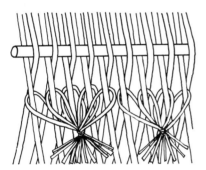

Diagram 66

Making the sheds: a simple frame and a frame with nails

Tapestry weaving is made in plain weave and so needs two sheds in the warp. On smaller frames there are several possible shedding devices, so you may need to try different methods depending on what you are weaving. Any of these methods work on frames with or without nails. See also p. 14 about making sheds.

Stick shed

The stick shed is the simplest device. A piece of dowel, called a stick or rod, is inserted over and under alternate warp ends to make a shed and remains in the warp throughout the weaving (Diag. 65a). The opposite shed is made with your fingers (Diag. 65b). Suitable for small frames and areas of tapestry with a lot of detail using different wefts.

Stick and grouped leashes

The stick and leash shed is the same as above, but the opposite shed has loops of cotton thread (leashes) attached to the warp ends *behind* the stick. Position the leashes below the stick in the warp and tie them together in groups of five or six (Diag. 66). Suitable for small to medium frames, enabling you to pull alternate warp ends forwards with the leashes instead of finding them with your fingers (Diag. 6 on p. 14). Some students find this method quicker, others prefer to find one shed by hand, so try it and see.

Rod and heddle sticks

This is ingenious, based on the Navajo Indian method of making sheds. There is a stick shed as in the first two methods above but then you make heddles (continuous loops of cotton), and attach them to another stick for the opposite shed. The instructions for making heddles are on p. 31. This method is suitable for designs where the weft travels from edge to edge, as in plain grounds and horizontal stripes, so if you want to weave simply designed functional things, for example mats, rugs or cushions, set up your sheds in this way. You will also need a shed stick for this method, to hold the shed open across the whole warp (see p. 53).

Sheds for a large frame

Leashes

Leashes, or lisses, are the traditional method by which weavers working on larger tapestries open one shed in the warp. They have been used on the vertical, high-warp frames since the Middle Ages. First pass a round stick through the warp in the natural shed, and line it up just above the leash bar clamped to the frame. Tie a length of cord tightly along the leash bar. Starting on the left of the leash bar, tie the end from a small ball of warp thread to the beginning of the cord with a half-hitch knot.

Take the ball of thread around the first warp end behind the stick in the warp, bring it up and over the leash bar and attach it to the cord with a double half-hitch. Now take the thread around the next warp end behind the stick, back up and over the leash bar and double hitch it to the cord again (Diag. 67).

Continue across the warp, keeping the leashes equal in length and fairly slack, and fasten off at the right end of the leash bar. By putting your hand behind a group of leashes and pulling downwards, the shed is forced open (Diag. 67 and Diag. 6 on p. 14). The opposite shed is always kept open by the stick in the warp.

Preparing the weft

Make butterflies of weft by winding yarn in a figure of eight between your thumb and little finger. Cut the yarn and loop the end around the centre of the butterfly in two half-hitches. The first end, which was looped around your thumb is the one you pull out and begin weaving with (Diag. 68).

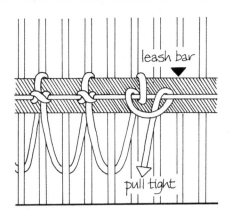

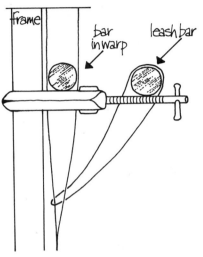

Diagram 67

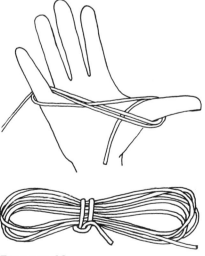

Diagram 68

Geometric patterns

I have divided the weaving techniques for tapestry into three sections: geometric patterns, texture and pictorial tapestry. The combination of these techniques should give you a thorough basis from which you can build and develop ideas of your own on the kind of tapestries you want to weave.

The first chapter, on geometric patterns, is an introduction to flat tapestry weave in which a variety of patterns can be woven using simple shapes. It covers the methods of weaving blocks, angles and circles using wefts which are horizontal to the warp, and is the foundation for the many patterns and geometric designs which can be so effective in tapestry.

There is a long tradition of flat-woven tapestry using colourful geometric patterns, best exemplified by the rugs and blankets from the Middle East, India, Central Europe, Scandinavia and North America. Contemporary weavers have found inspiration from these traditional patterns, and have developed geometric designs into bold and striking pieces of weaving, with clean, sharp images and strong colours. Attractive combinations of colour and geometrical shapes can be used not only when weaving functional items such as rugs, cushions, bags etc, but can also be a way of expressing individual ideas in tapestry. The horizontal and vertical structure of weaving can really be exploited to the full with geometric designs, and the marrying together of pattern, colour and the tactile surface texture of the weave can make this a very exciting and dramatic form of tapestry.

Detail from a geometrically patterned wall-hanging. The tassels and shaped edge help to counterbalance the repeating horizontal patterns. Woven by the author.

Plain weave

The weave structure of tapestry is a weft-faced plain weave, (see Diag. 1 p.9). The weft covers the warp completely and must be set in loosely and beaten down firmly.

As I described in 'About weaving', p. 8, plain weave consists of two alternating rows. The weft passes over alternate warp ends in one row then returns over the opposite alternate warp ends in the next row. In tapestry these two rows are called a pass (Diag. 69) and one row a half-pass. It is very important to keep the weft slack when passing it through the shed so that it can be beaten down easily. Getting an even weave, not too tight so the weaving pulls in nor too loose so the surface is uneven and bubbly, is something which comes with practice. Always arc the weft when you have passed it through the shed, allowing it to feed into the shed quite loosely, and then beat it down firmly with the beater. The weft should curve gently around each warp end. Turn the weft at the edges neatly and if the weaving droops at the edges, make an extra turn on every few rows (Diag. 69).

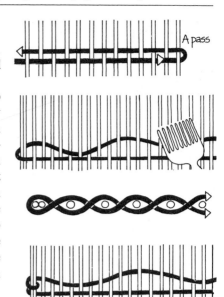

Diagram 69

Starting and finishing ends of weft

Because tapestry is built up from a number of shapes in different coloured yarns, you need separate butterflies of yarn for each shape you are weaving (see p.59). This results in a great many ends of yarn on the wrong side of the weaving, and so it is important to begin and end each end correctly and securely. Begin each new weft by tucking the end, about 6 cm (2½ in) long, to the back of the weaving as shown in Diag. 70. How you do this will depend on which shed you are in. This method is the same when you run out of weft and need to join in a new length of yarn. If you are using several fine strands of yarn twisted together as one weft, then tuck all the strands together to the back. These ends will be secure if you pack the weaving down firmly. When the weaving is finished you can darn in the ends at the back if you want a very neat finish, or alternatively they can be left loose if you are going to back the tapestry, (see p. 94.).

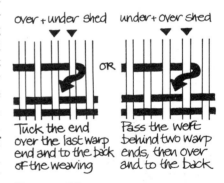

Tuck the end over the last warp end and to the back of the weaving

Pass the weft behind two warp ends, then over and to the back

Diagram 70

The above method is most suitable for tapestries you are going to hang up, or for cushions or bags which will be lined, but for rugs where both sides need to be perfect there is an alternative, which is to join the wefts by overlapping them in the shed as you weave. It is much easier to do this if you are working with doubled wefts, which is usual for rugs, but if the weft is only a single strand such as 2-ply rug yarn, then split the ply. Separate the strands of weft and pull ends about 6 cm (2½ in) long out of the shed at different places in the warp. Overlap the new weft in the same shed (Diag. 71). These ends can then be darned vertically into the weave and trimmed.

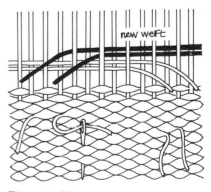

Diagram 71

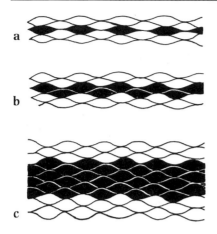

Diagram 72

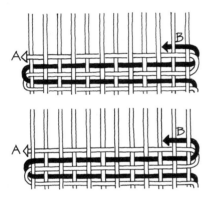

Diagram 73

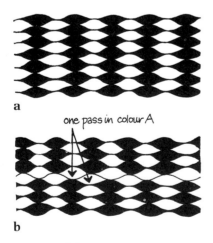

Diagram 74

Stripes

Horizontal stripes
It is very simple to build up stripes in plain weave with different coloured yarns, but it is important to avoid having ends of yarns at the edges of the weaving. Always change from one colour to the next by joining the ends about four warp ends from the edge at the end of one half-pass or the beginning of the next. One half-pass of a different colour will make a line of spots (Diag. 72a). One pass of a different weft will make a thin wavy line (Diag. 72b). For thicker stripes, weave a number of passes to the depth you want (Diag. 72c).

Vertical stripes
Vertical stripes are created in the weave by alternating a half-pass in one colour with a half-pass in another colour. To avoid ends of weft at the edges a continuous weft is passed through alternate sheds, but in the *same* direction across the warp. Take colour A through the shed from left to right, then take colour B through the opposite shed but again from left to right. Pick up colour A again, pass it *over* colour B at the edge if you are weaving behind the first warp end, or *under* colour B if you are weaving in front of the first warp end (Diag. 73). Colour A is then locked firmly at the edge so it won't pull back. Pick up colour B and weave it through the next shed. Repeat this when you turn colour A around again. The vertical stripes build up in the weave because the same colour is continuously passing over the same alternate warp ends in every alternate row (Diag. 74a). You can counterchange the position of the colours to make a check pattern by weaving one pass, (two rows) in the same colour and then reverting to half-passes in two different colours (Diag. 74b).

Separate blocks of colour

Each block needs a separate coloured weft, so first of all calculate how many blocks you are going to weave across the width of the warp and how many warp ends each block will need. If you have worked out a design and drawn a cartoon whch is positioned behind the warp (see p. 91), then you can see the outline of each block clearly. Otherwise mark the warp ends you will be turning on with coloured felt pens. You will need a separate butterfly of yarn for each block in the pattern. To avoid confusion with so many wefts I think it is easier initially to weave each weft in the same direction in any one row. This isn't a hard and fast rule as there are patterns which have wefts opposing one another, but I have described this on p. 66 where the wefts are joined. For separate blocks, direction of the wefts isn't especially important.

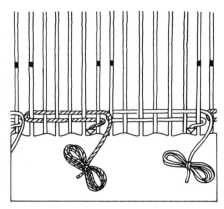

Diagram 75

Set in the end of weft at the beginning of each block, either around all the right or the left warp ends. Weave a pass with each weft, all in the same shed (Diag. 75). The wefts are woven separately to build up each block. You can do this in two ways; open the shed across the whole width of the warp using a shed stick to hold it open and pass each weft across each block, in the same direction, and beat all the wefts down. Change the shed and weave in the opposite direction. I find a quicker way is to weave each shape completely to the depth required, and then move across to the next shape. This method of building up shapes successively in different areas of the warp is really true tapestry. Remember when gauging the depth of a shape that the weaving will contract as it is beaten down so always weave two or three half-passes above the line of the cartoon, or your planned size, to allow for this.

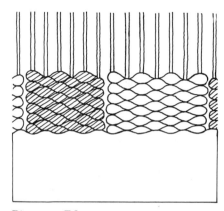

Diagram 76

Weaving blocks separately in this way results in slits in the weaving between each shape (Diag. 76). These slits can be a feature of the weave by giving form and definition to the patterns, or by being an integral part of the design (see kilim, p. 68). Too many long slits can create weaknesses in the fabric if it is to have any practical purpose. However, slits can be very striking when planned as part of the design—for example, in a wall hanging, where the spaces created add interest visually to the whole piece.

Take care with the tension of the wefts when weaving separate shapes. The weft has to be slack in tapestry but at the same time you should not turn it too loosely at the edges or the shapes will bulge outwards. Neither must it be too tight or the slits will become holes. With practice you will achieve the correct tension. A good guide is to think that 'the smaller the shape, the tighter the weft.'

Slits in the weaving can, if desired, be sewn up afterwards with a fine weft or invisible thread (Diag. 77). Take care not to pull the weaving in if you do this. Sewing up slits is most suitable for shapes in the weave where there needs to be a sharp division between one vertical edge and another with no visible sign of a join.

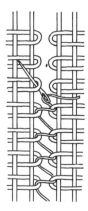

Diagram 77

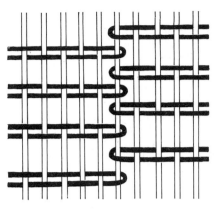

Diagram 78

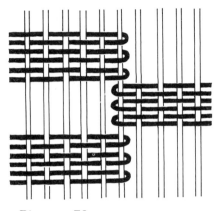

Diagram 79

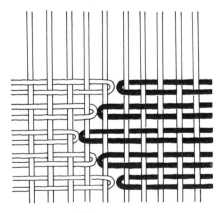

Diagram 80

Joining separate blocks

Dovetailing

One way to avoid slits between separate areas of colour in tapestry is to make the wefts from adjacent areas turn around a common warp end. Diag. 78 shows how each weft from first one side then the other is taken across the warp and back around the same warp end. In order to do this the wefts in each shape must be woven in opposing directions.

The vertical dovetail can make a single turn with each alternate weft (Diag. 78) or can be a double or triple turn (Diag. 79). The result in all cases is a jagged tooth-edged join. Paradoxically the triple turning dovetail beats down more successfully than the single turn as the toothed-edges lock into one another more neatly. Because dovetailing is such a visible join, consider where this can best be used for colour joining and make a feature of it.

An angled dovetail is an alternative join where the wefts don't build up in one place but are staggered diagonally. In this join the wefts do not turn around a common warp end but turn consecutively around three warp ends, first in one direction then in the other (Diag. 80). As with the vertical dovetail the wefts must pass through the warp in opposing directions. The first weft A is carried across and back, then the adjacent weft B is carried across and back, each turning on adjacent warp ends. The first weft A is then brought across one warp end further and turned around. Then weft B comes across, turns on the adjacent warp end and moves back. Finally weft A turns on one warp end further again and moves back, and weft B is brought across to meet it and return. This sequence is then reversed so the B weft increases into the area of the A weft.

Colour plate:
Tapestry woven wall-hanging using geometric patterns and rich colours. Woven by the author.

Interlocking

This join is made by looping two adjacent wefts around one another in the space between two adjacent warp ends (Diag. 81). It can be used between vertical edges, as a staggered join and in any position in the weaving where there might otherwise be a weak point. If the tension of the wefts is correct it is only slightly visible. It can be carried out when wefts are passed through the warp in opposing directions or continuously in one direction, but all must be in the same shed.

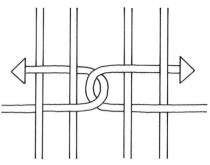

Diagram 81

Interlocking wefts which move in the same direction

Diag. 82 shows the steps in interlocking wefts between two adjacent shapes. The wefts are set into the warp so they move in the same direction. Follow steps 1 to 4 below to understand how the interlock is made. The interlocking join does not have to be made on every half-pass in the weaving, as it can become rather bulky if you do. I tend to weave a complete pass between each interlocking row and this holds the shapes in the weaving together sufficiently. Diag. 82 only indicates how to join two adjacent shapes together. If however you want to weave a series of interlocked shapes across the width of the warp, you will need to weave each shape row by row as follows:

1 Set in the wefts from left to right as in step a. Starting on the right weave all wefts from right to left, so you are following step b with the first weft and then each successive weft loops around the previous one and moves to the left as in step c.
2 Starting on the left now move all the wefts to the right to hold the interlock, as in step d. Check the tension of the interlock, making sure it is in the middle of the space between adjacent warp ends.
3 Starting on the right move all the wefts to the left (no interlock on this row).
4 Starting on the left move all the wefts to the right (no interlock on this row). Then repeat steps a to d.

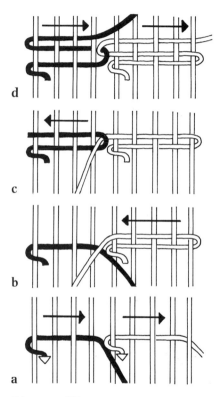

Diagram 82

Colour plate:
A small weaving frame with nails is ideal for trying out small samples and projects in tapestry. This frame has hinges so it can stand upright on a table and makes weaving and assessing the work in progress easier.

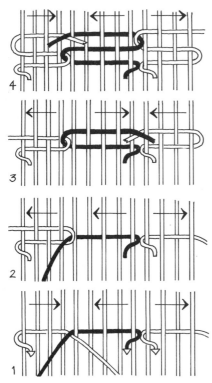

Diagram 83

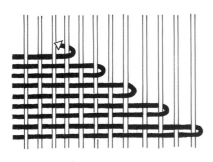

Diagram 84

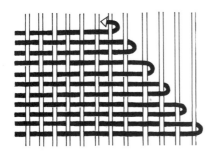

Diagram 85

Interlocking wefts which move in opposite directions

Diag. 83 shows how wefts can be interlocked when moving in opposite directions. Always keep the direction of the loop the same with each successive interlock so the joins are neat when pushed down. If, after the interlock, one weft has to make a diagonal jump over the other into the shed for the next row, then you have looped the wefts around one another the wrong way. With practice you will see that the interlocked wefts should be horizontal to the warp when pushed down. With this continuous interlocking, it seems easier to loop the wefts at each join on every row. If this is too bulky, however, make one or two turns without interlocking in between the rows where you do make a join.

Apart from interlocking wefts on adjacent shapes with vertical edges, this join can be made at any junction of wefts if by doing so an unsightly gap, however small, can be avoided. One very important thing to bear in mind is the correct tension of the wefts. I have already mentioned the importance of keeping the weft slack in the shed so it can be beaten down firmly. However, the interlocked wefts need to be pulled tightly to ensure the join is centred between the warp ends. This contradiction can be overcome if you tighten the wefts at the join, push the join down, arc the wefts through the rest of the shed and beat them firmly.

Triangles and angled shapes

Weaving square blocks is relatively straightforward because the wefts always turn around on the same warp ends. With angled shapes, however, you will need to increase or decrease the number of warp ends you are weaving on.

Controlling the angles

The angle of a shape is controlled by three factors: the number of passes the weft makes, the number of warp ends to the centimetre (or inch) and the regularity with which the weft decreases or increases round the warp ends. Diags. 84 and 85 show how different angles can be made by decreasing on every other warp end, and on every single warp end, both using the same warp spacing and thickness of weft.

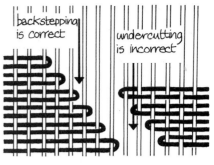

Diagram 86

Backstepping

Because tapestry is built up in separate areas it is important to understand which areas to deal with first. With triangles, diamonds and any angled shapes always follow the principle of weaving the shape with the receding edge first. With a triangle it can be two receding edges being woven simultaneously. This method is known as backstepping (Diag. 86) and logically then allows you to weave the adjacent shape, so it can lock into the receding one. If you were to undercut, that is to weave an extending shape first, the shape would collapse as it would have no base and it would be impossible to open the shed to weave the area beneath it (Diag. 86). Diag. 87 shows the order in which to approach an angled design.

Weaving a triangle

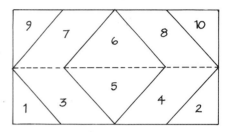

Diagram 87

You will first need to decide the angles of your triangle and the width of the base. The cartoon behind the warp will guide you, or you can mark a triangle onto the warp ends with a felt pen (see p. 93). I prefer to have an odd number of warp ends at the base so the triangle will decrease to a single warp end, thus giving it a good point. You can begin with an even number, though, and decrease to two warp ends.

The number of passes you weave is guided by the angle you have drawn, so you can see when to decrease (Diag. 88). Remember, the weaving packs down, so weave slightly above the guideline. If you are weaving several triangles in a row, weave each one in turn with its separate weft. If you finish on a single warp end, darn the end down into the back of the weaving. Having woven the upright triangle, then weave the adjacent areas, but this time weave around an increasing number of warp ends, making sure that the number of passes is exactly the same as before so the shapes fit neatly into one another.

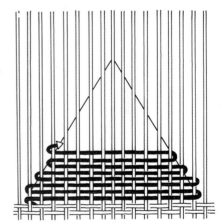

Diagram 88

Lazy lines

When you are weaving a large area of one colour it is much quicker and easier to break it up into smaller shapes and weave them individually, rather than carrying a single weft across the full width and back. This particularly applies to larger tapestries. A part of the whole area is begun by weaving an angled shape, backstepping as you weave. Another shape can then be over-laid against the first one, woven with a separate weft. Gradually the whole area is built up and because it consists of several small shapes, the edges of these shapes show as faint lines in the one colour area and are known as lazy lines. Diag. 89 gives an idea of how a large area in one colour can be divided and woven in this way.

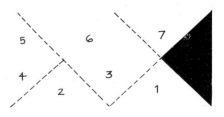

Diagram 89

Detail from a traditional Turkish kilim woven bag. The individual motifs are made by stepping the wefts. It is the way the motifs are linked together which produce the intricate geometric design.

Kilim

Kilim, or kelim, is derived from an Arabic word and has become commonly used as a description for Middle-Eastern flat-woven rugs, blankets and saddle-bags. Traditionally associated with the Arab tribes of Asia Minor, who produced kilims for their own use as furnishings for their tents and for wrapping and carrying their goods, this type of weaving has an unsophisticated appeal which has only become appreciated in the West in the last fifty years or so. Long overshadowed by the elaborate high-court knotted carpets, and in fact often used simply to wrap up the carpets for transportation, kilims are now recognised as equally fine textile works. The kilim has flourished in the Middle East for over 4000 years, but it is also highly developed in India, Central Europe, particularly the Caucasus and the Balkan region, and Sweden and Finland.

The word kilim is not only a general term for textiles from the Middle East and other regions. Originally it was the description of the weaving technique. The essential characteristic of the kilim technique is that individual shapes in mainly geometric designs are built up with separate wefts, creating a detailed juxtaposition of colours and patterns. Since no weft passes from selvedge to selvedge the resulting weave has tiny vertical slits between the pattern areas, and this is the recognisable feature of kilim. To avoid overlong slits, the patterns are typically intricate with indented edges, and the design is equally clear on both sides of the weaving (see photo).

Kilim patterns

The traditional patterns in kilims are based on geometric shapes using rich colours woven into intricate designs. The shapes invariably have indented, or stepped, edges. Designs for kilims can be based on triangles, angled shapes, diamonds, squares, rectangles and lozenge shapes. Diag. 90, for example, shows a simple motif based on rectangular blocks. This motif can be repeated and inverted to make a complete kilim design. Each block is built up individually with separate wefts.

Indented blocks

There are two ways you can weave this pattern. In either case the separate wefts all travel in the same direction.

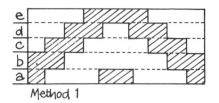

Method 1

Diagram 90

Method 1

The motif is divided into horizontal bands a to e (Diag. 90). Within each band a different number of wefts are needed. In band a five different coloured wefts should be set in across the warp to the appropriate number of warp ends. Build up each block of colour to the depth you want. At the beginning of band b the wefts must be re-arranged in the following way:

1 After completing band a with a half-pass from right to left, leave weft 1 on the left and push wefts 2 to 5 to the back.
2 For band b weave weft 1 to the right plus two warp ends more than before. Bring weft 2 from the back, weave it across 3 and 4 but stop two warp ends less than before. Bring weft 5 to the front and first take it two warp ends to the left, then weave it across to the right edge (Diag. 91).

This completes the re-arrangement of wefts for band b in which you will use three wefts. However, where weft 5 began (Diag. 91, point X), you will see there are two wefts in the same shed.

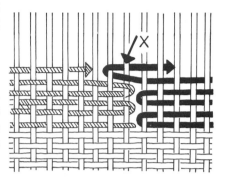

Diagram 91

Problems caused by wefts in the same shed

The problem with this method is that at the place where the wefts change position there are two wefts in the same shed. Subsequent wefts will pack down to cover the fault unless the weft is thick, in which case the warp will show through. The alternative is to pass weft 5 behind the warp where it changes position and then weave it across to the right (Diag. 92). This can only be done if you are changing position by an even number of warp ends. The loop this makes on the back of the weaving is acceptable for a tapestry you are going to back or hang up. If, however, your weaving needs to be as neat on the front as the back (with rugs, for example) then the method shown in Diag. 91 is the only choice. Compensate for the fault by making an extra weft turn around the warp end which the weft wouldn't cover in the normal sheds.

Continue to weave each band as shown in Diag. 90, ending each one with all the wefts in the same direction, in the same shed, and then re-arrange them in a similar way to bands a and b.

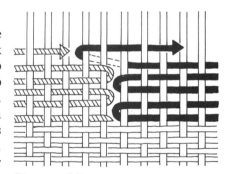

Diagram 92

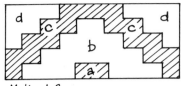

Method 2

Diagram 93

Method 2

Here the blocks of colour are built up in a different sequence, (Diag. 93) but the method of re-arranging the wefts is the same as in method 1.

1 Start in the centre with shape a and weave it completely.
2 Shape b needs two wefts to begin with, either side of a, so start with both wefts travelling in the same direction and in the same shed as a. When you are level with the top of a, put the right b weft to the back.
3 Starting on the left weave right across over a, and stop two warp ends less on the right than before. Return with the same weft but stop two warp ends less on the left. Now start to build up shape b on this number of warp ends. Continue, stepping in the edges as you go till you have reached the top of b.
4 Now introduce a weft for the right side of shape c. When it reaches the first indentation in shape b, re-arrange its position by one of the methods on p. 69. Keep building up shape c step by step so it fits into b, then move across to the left of shape c and weave that with a separate weft in the same way.
5 Complete the motif by filling in shapes d on the right and left.

Navajo wedge-weave

This is a technique originated by the Navajo Indians in North America, to weave the vibrant zig-zag patterns in their blankets.

It is a unique method in which the weft is woven diagonally to the warp. If a complete piece of weaving is made in this technique, there is a tendency for the warp to become distorted so take care to keep the tension of the weft fairly loose. You can counteract any problems with the warp by placing stripes of horizontal weaving between the wedge-weave to re-align the warp spacing.

Wedge-weave is the most effective way of weaving diagonal stripes and zig-zag patterns because it produces shapes with smooth clean edges, unlike the method of weaving diagonals with horizontal wefts which results in stepped edges as the wefts decrease and increase on the warp ends.

Begin on the right edge of the warp and weave a triangle with a right-angled edge against the edge of the warp. The sloping side of the triangle will dictate the angle at which all the diagonal stripes will be, so don't make it too steep or you will have problems with a distorted warp. I would suggest that if you are weaving on a warp of four ends per 2.5 cm (1 in), the base of the triangle should cover seven warp ends, decreasing to one at the top right, with two passes on each number of warp ends before you increase.

1 Set in the weft on the first two warp ends at the right of the warp, and weave from left to right so your end is tucked into the second warp space, not on the outer edge.

2 Weave two passes on warp ends 1 and 2 and increase to 3 on the last half-pass (Diag. 94).

3 Weave two passes on warp ends 1 to 3 and increase to 4 on the last half-pass (Diag. 95). Keep the weft loose, especially at the base, as the weft has to be pushed down to the horizontal level of the stripe below or there will be holes in the weaving.

4 Continue in this way, increasing one warp end on every fourth half-pass, pushing the weaving down carefully as it becomes more diagonal. Finish by taking the weft up to the top after completing two passes on warps 1 to 7. Leave the butterfly of weft at the top for later.

5 Change to a different coloured weft for the first stripe or wedge. Starting at the top on warp 2, weave two passes from 2 at the top to warp 8 at the bottom.

6 Increase to warp ends 3 and 9 (Diag. 96). When your wedge is as wide as you want, leave the weft at the top for later, and start a new colour on the next warp end. Your wedges can be as narrow as one warp end or several warp ends wide.

7 When you are seven warp ends from the left edge at the top of the wedges, weave a triangle as you did as the beginning, except the process is reversed by decreasing from warp 7 to the last two.

You have now woven a band of wedges across the warp. Pick up each weft in turn and weave from left to right, and this time the first triangle will have its right-angled edge against the left edge of the warp, so all the wedges will be angled the opposite way (Diag. 97). Try to wind enough weft for each coloured wedge, but if you run out join in a new weft on the diagonal edge as you would for horizontal tapestry (see p. 61).

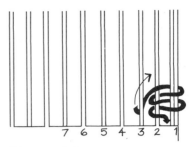

Diagram 94

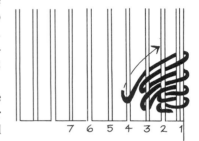

Diagram 95

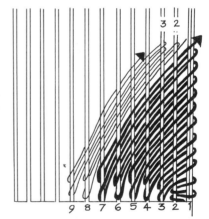

Diagram 96

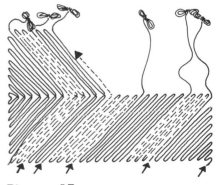

Diagram 97

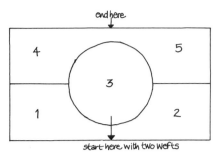

Diagram 98

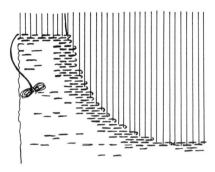

Diagram 99

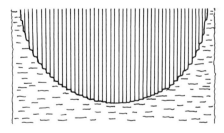

Diagram 100

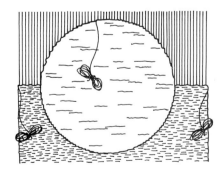

Diagram 101

Circles and curved shapes

Weaving circular and curved shapes are the most difficult in tapestry simply because of the direction of the warp and weft. It is always very helpful to have the shape you want to interpret either on the cartoon, or inked onto the warp itself.

I will concentrate here on using wefts which pass through the warp horizontally, which means that in order to give the effect of curves the weft needs to be stepped gradually, following the outline of the shape. There are other techniques in tapestry using curved wefts and these are dealt with fully in 'pictorial tapestry' on p. 85.

Weaving a circle

Diag. 98 shows the steps in weaving a plain circle on a contrasting background. You will need two butterflies of weft, the colour of the background, and you begin with these in the centre of the warp, taking each weft out to the edges in the same shed. Weave a few passes with the wefts meeting and separating in the centre of the warp (see hatching, p. 88).

Starting on the left with the left-hand weft, weave it across to the centre and turn it around on the first warp end where the line begins to curve upwards. Take the weft out to the left and then return to the centre, again turning on the warp end closest to the curved line. Continue to build up the background area on the left, taking care to follow the curve as accurately as you can, and remembering to allow for the fact that the weaving will pack down (Diag. 99). At the base of the curve the weft may only turn on every three or four warp ends after each pass, but as the incline of the curve becomes sharper you may need to turn several times on one warp end before you decrease to the next one. When you have reached halfway up the circle with the left background area, leave the weft for later and start on the right side, matching it to the left curve as evenly as you can. Stop when you are halfway as you did on the left (Diag. 100).

Now introduce the weft for the circle itself at the base of the curve. If it is a large circle, begin with two wefts as you did with the background and meet and separate them. Build up the circle, taking care to increase neatly into the curved edge of the background area. At the halfway level continue the circle, this time decreasing on either side (Diag. 101). You may need quite a few passes across the circle at the halfway level, or it will pack down to an oval shape.

Finally build up the left and right background areas with separate wefts, finishing the ends in the centre in the same shed.

High and low passes

Because we are concerned with trying to weave curved edges which look as smooth as possible, it is important to say something here about how the weft turns around on the warp end when increasing and decreasing shapes. This also applies to shapes which need to have smooth angular edges.

Depending on which shed the weft is in, it will turn differently around a warp end, either passing in front of the warp end at the beginning of a new pass (Diag. 102a) or behind the warp end (Diag. 102b). As you can see from the diagrams, when the weft is beaten down the end result is quite different. In Diag. 102a the turn is quite rounded and bumpy and is called a high pass, whereas in Diag. 102b the low pass gives a smoother, flatter turn. In order to weave shapes with diagonal or curved edges, the weft is successively turned around single warp ends in a certain sequence, and it becomes clear that if most of the turns are high passes, the edge will be a lot bumpier than if there are more of the smoother low passes.

This does not mean that you only attempt to weave low passes. It is the edge of the shape which you follow first and foremost. The important thing is to be aware of high and low passes and to exploit them fully, so that (for example) within a given number of warp ends in which you are weaving a curve, you make more low passes and less high passes, so the weaving results in a smooth edge when beaten down.

a

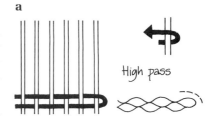

High pass

b

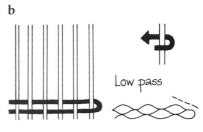

Low pass

Diagram 102

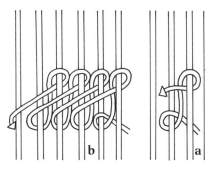

Diagram 106

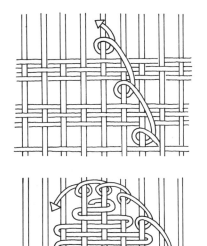

Diagram 107

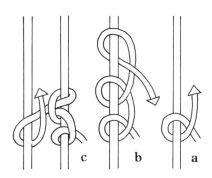

Diagram 108

Double soumak
Double soumak is locked into a very firm ridge and is made by looping forwards over two warp ends then back over one in a figure of eight (Diag. 106).

Outlining with soumak
Soumak can be worked at an angle to the warp as well as horizontally and when it is done in this way it is often used to outline a shape, or to create diagonal surface decoration. It is often found in kilims, where it emphasises certain motifs.

Diag. 107 shows how soumak can be made to loop over passes of plain weave. Beat the weaving down as you work, and take care that the soumak loops are neither too tight nor too slack. Diag. 107 also shows how to outline a shape. Weave the triangle first, (see p. 67) then soumak around it. The surrounding areas are then built up with plain weave.

Greek soumak
Greek soumak produces a very thick weave which has an interesting texture on both sides, so can be reversed depending on the effect you want. Diag. 108 illustrates the method and if this is worked from the front of the warp the result is a chevron pattern. The back appears as a vertical ribbing. Unlike the previous soumaks, the Greek one can be worked over the entire warp or in large areas without the necessity to do plain weave in between. Because of this it produces a firm textile which would be suitable for making practical, hard-wearing articles.

Twining

Twining, one of the earliest methods of interlacing fibres, was first used in basket-making in primitive cultures, and then became a textile technique. In the history of textiles is certainly seems to pre-date woven cloth, but because the process consisted of twisting one set of fibres through another set held in tension, it was probably the first step to weaving.

Evidence of weft-twining has been found in textiles from Ancient Peru, Anatolia, the Chilkat blankets from the Pacific coast of North America and the cloaks made by the Maoris in New Zealand, so it was a universal technique. On p. 56 I have described the functional use of twining as a very efficient method of spacing the warp evenly, but it can also be used as a decorative technique in tapestry, especially when the wefts are different colours.

Diag. 109a shows the construction of weft-twining. If the two wefts are different colours, then a variety of patterns can be produced. The patterns are made by the direction of the twist and the way the coloured wefts are arranged in each successive row. Diag. 109b shows the S twist and 109c the Z twist. Twining can make an S twist alternating with a row in a Z twist, or the two wefts can repeatedly make S twists or Z twists. As the wefts turn on the end of each row you can make an extra twist to enable the colours to appear in line with the previous row, as in Diag. 109d, or you can counterchange the position of the colours, as in Diag. 109e. Twining in a light colour makes an interesting surface texture, especially when contrasted with plain weave. The alternating S and Z twist rows look very similar to single soumak worked at reversed angles. Start and finish the ends of the wefts by darning them into the back of the weave.

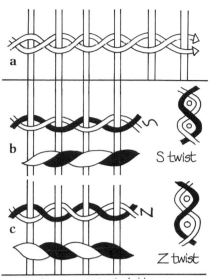

S twist

Z twist

Alternating rows of S and Z twist: black above black, white above white

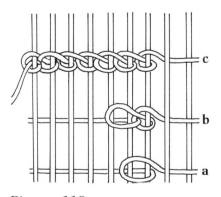

white above black, black above white

Diagram 109

Chaining

Chaining is another technique which can be used decoratively like soumak and also needs at least one pass of plain weave between each row of chaining. Its appearance is very like chain stitch in embroidery.

Introduce the chaining weft into the warp and darn the end in securely at the back. Weave three or four warp ends then pass the entire weft behind the warp. Pull a loop from the weft forward in the space between the next two warp ends (Diag. 110a). Put your fingers through the loop and pull on the weft behind the warp, so you are pulling another loop through the existing one in the next space along the warp (Diag. 110b). Continue in this way, pulling another loop from the weft through each chain in each successive warp space, tightening each loop as you go. As you move across the warp the loops get larger so keep them all even by pulling on the weft behind the warp. Complete the row by bringing the end through the last loop in the chain (Diag. 110c). As with soumak, you can use the same weft for plain weave, or work the chaining row and the plain weave with separate wefts (see p. 75).

Diagram 110

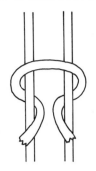

Diagram 111

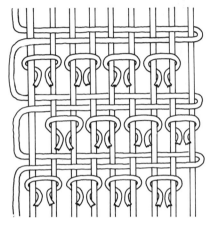

Diagram 112

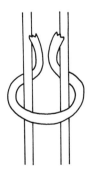

Diagram 113

Knots

The use of knots to produce pile fabrics has had an interesting and varied history, with early beginnings. Some of the finest knotted textiles were the richly patterned carpets of the East, particularly in Persia, Turkey, the Caucasus, Turkestan and China. In Scandinavia, the traditional rya rugs, with their long shaggy pile knotted on both sides, were made for extra warmth and a luxurious feel.

Knotting consists of looping cut lengths of wool, silk or cotton around two adjacent warp ends so the fibres protrude, creating a pile. Between the rows of knots is a pass of plain weave, and the combination of these produces a thick, heavy textile which is very hard-wearing. Because each knot can be a different colour the design possibilities of this technique are infinite, and the most intricate patterns can be produced. In different parts of the world where knotting is used, carpets from particular regions use distinctive colours and types of knots, and the length of the knots and the density also varies considerably. In contemporary weaving knotting has been used with tapestry and other techniques to make textiles which are functional, such as rugs, as well as decorative hangings and sculptures.

Although there are many different types of knots, I will concentrate here on four classic ones.

Ghiordes knot

The Ghiordes or Turkish knot is a very firm knot and is probably the most widely used today. Prepare cut yarns of equal length. I do this by winding the yarn around a small book and then cutting it at each edge. The length of your knots is a personal choice but at first you may find it easier to err on the generous side, so you are able to make the knots easily, and then trim them to the finished pile length afterwards. Lengths of about 7.5 cm (3 in) are quite practical to work with.

Diag. 111 shows how the knot is made. It can consist of a single length of rug yarn, or can be double or tripled, or can be finer or different textured yarns stranded together. You can gradually change the tones of colour over a knotted area by mixing colours in the strands of yarn.

After a completed row of knots it is essential to make at least one pass in plain weave, beating it down firmly to hold the knots in place. The following row of knots is then made on the alternate pairs of warp ends, so the pile is evenly distributed (Diag. 112). When the knot is made in this way, the direction of the pile slopes downwards. To make the pile stand out from the surface of the weave, make two or three rows of reversed knots at the beginning of the knotted area (Diag. 113). This will then prevent the pile from flattening down.

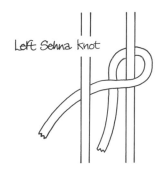

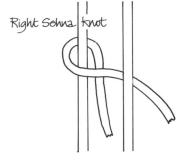

Diagram 114   Diagram 115

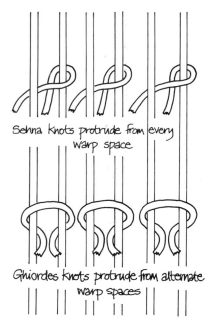

Diagram 116

Sehna knot

The Sehna or Persian knot is also tied around two warp ends, but it is asymmetrical, unlike the Ghiordes knot which is symmetrical. It has been used in Persia, India and Egypt and in some of the court rugs in Turkey.

The figure of eight twist made by the Sehna knot can create a pile which faces to the left (Diag. 114) or to the right (Diag. 115). Because the ends of the Sehna knot protrude between all the warp spaces, unlike the Ghiordes knot which does so only between alternate spaces, it can produce very dense areas of knotting (Diag. 116). This is why the Persian court carpets have such a compact pile with very intricately detailed designs.

Prepare cut lengths of yarn for Sehna knots in the same way as for Ghiordes knots, and weave a pass of plain weave between each row of knots. Tie the knots on alternate warp ends in each consecutive row but concentrate on either a left or right-hand Sehna.

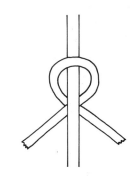

Diagram 117

Spanish knot

The Arabs ruled Spain for much of the Middle Ages and it was largely through their influence that knotted carpets were made in Spain. The Spanish knot is tied around every alternate warp end (Diag. 117). The ends of the knot protrude either side of the warp end, with the adjacent warp ends either side left unknotted. Each successive row of knots is made on the opposite warp ends with three half-passes of plain weave in between, in alternating sheds, which cover the warp when beaten down (Diag. 118).

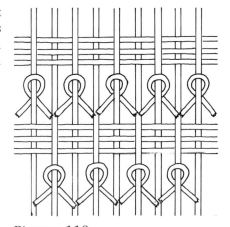

Diagram 118

Rya

Rya rugs, or ryijis, seem to date from the fifteenth century, and were made as bedcovers in Scandinavia. Traditional ryas have a pile of long, shaggy knots on both sides, undoubtedly made in this way to create warmth and to give a luxurious feel. They were usually made for the daughter of a family as part of her dowry, to be used to cover the marriage bed, and the custom was also to use the rya as a wedding rug on which the couple stood while the marriage ceremony took place.

The knot used for Rya is the same as the Ghiordes knot, but it is looped around the first and third warp ends and so on, facing upwards, then the knot facing downwards loops around the second and fourth warp ends, and so on. Between each row of knots there are three half-passes of plain weave, as in the Spanish method.

Loops

Making loops with the weft is another way of adding texture to a piece of tapestry weaving. They can be made by pulling up the weft as it is passed through the shed, thus making pulled loops, or with an additional weft which is taken around the warp ends in the same way as the knots already described, as wrapped loops. It has been suggested that in some early textiles the method of pulled loops, or of making loops with a continuous weft wrapped around the warp and subsequently cut to create pile, preceded the technique of knotting with cut lengths of yarn. In fact many carpets are still made in this way, and the dexterity of an experienced weaver is such that he or she can very rapidly make loops around the warp from a continuous ball of yarn while holding a pair of shears in the other hand with which to clip the loops at the end of each row.

On the whole wrapped loops are stronger than pulled loops as the latter can slip to the back of the weaving if not firmly packed down. This section begins with wrapped loops which, as you will see, are wrapped around the warp in the same way as some of the knots already described.

Colour plate:
Simple stepped geometric patterns can be used to create intricate designs.

Main picture: Traditional Turkish kelim woven as a saddle-bag.
Inset: Small panel, echoing the design of the traditional Middle Eastern prayer mats. Woven by the author.

The use of the meet and separate technique in tapestry and additional wrapping make this picture of a tree set against the sky very effective and dramatic. Woven by Maggie Stewart.

Landscape scenes can be interpreted very successfully in tapestry. Here meet and separate technique was used for the sea and sky, and soumak, Greek knots and looping for the cliffs. Woven by Adrienne Tufnail.

Ghiordes loop

The Ghiordes loop has the same structure as the knot. All loops are made continuously with one weft which is joined into the weaving in the same way as a normal weft (see p. 61). With this loop you will need a thin stick or pencil around which the weft is passed. This acts as a gauge and enables you to make loops of equal length.

Start by joining in the weft on the right. Hold the stick in front of the warp in the position where you are going to make the row of loops. Bring the weft over the stick and behind the first warp end (Diag. 119a). Then take the weft across to the next warp end, pass it in front of the warp end, around and behind it, and bring the weft out underneath the stick again (Diag. 119b). Now make a second loop on the next two warp ends. Continue until your row of loops is complete (Diag. 119c), then pull out the stick. The width of the stick obviously dictates the length of the loops, so use a broader stick for longer loops. Reverse the direction of loops made from left to right. After each row, make a pass in plain weave, using a separate weft. Each successive row of loops should be made on alternate pairs of warp ends to the previous row.

The Ghiordes loops can be cut to make knots, so this could be an alternative method of knotting, as already mentioned. The loops can also be made in doubled yarn, for extra thickness, or for a weaving which needs textural interest, use bouclé, gimp or slub yarns.

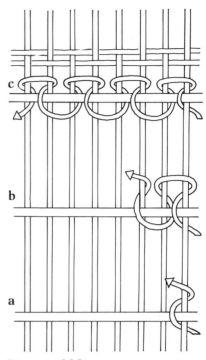

Diagram 119

Egyptian loop

I have included the Egyptian loop here, although strictly speaking it does not make a loop which stands out from the surface of the weave. It is, however, a valuable addition to the weaver's vocabulary of techniques.

The Egyptian loop produces an interesting vertical rib effect with a firm, fairly flat texture. It does not need a pass of plain weave between each row, but can be built up solidly over an area. It takes several rows to appreciate its ribbed pattern and it can be very effective when used next to areas of plain weave. Diag. 120 shows the Egyptian loop worked from right to left. The following row is worked continuously from left to right. The back of two rows of Egyptian loops looks exactly like two rows of single soumak worked in reversed angles (see p. 75).

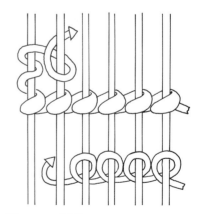

Diagram 120

Colour plate:
Some of the early fifteenth century tapestries show how superbly figures can be woven in tapestry, achieving great detail with careful shading of a limited range of colours. Detail from the courting scene from 'Falconry', one of the *Devonshire Hunting Tapestries. c.* 1430. Courtesy of the Victoria and Albert Museum, London.

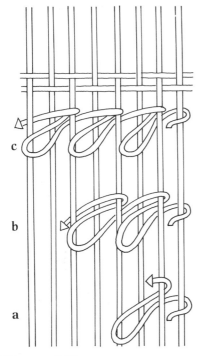

Diagram 121

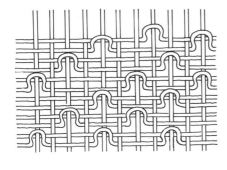

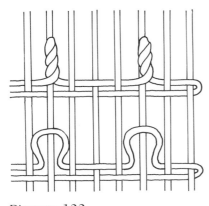

Diagram 122

Sehna loop

The Sehna loop is like the knot and can be used to make continuous loops or can be cut afterwards to make pile. The loop is made around alternate warp ends.

Start by joining in the weft on the right. Pass the weft behind the next warp end, make a loop and pass the weft back behind the same warp end and around it (Diag. 121a). Take the weft over the next warp end and behind the one after. Make another loop around this warp end, and continue (Diag. 121b and c).

Between each row of loops make a pass in plain weave, then work another row of loops on the opposite warp ends to the previous row. To make loops which are like the right-hand Sehna knot, that is, loops which slope downwards to the right, begin the weft on the left of the weaving.

Pulled loops

Pulled loops, sometimes called pulled wefts, or tufting, differ from the wrapped loops already described in that they are made by pulling on the weft which is carried through the normal sheds for plain weaving. In some early weaving, particularly in Ancient Egypt, the looped areas were in a contrasting colour, introduced into the warp much like the different wefts are in tapestry, so the motifs stood out from a plain woven ground. Join in the weft and make one half-pass. Keep the weft slack, and starting near the beginning of the row, pull up the weft into loops between every second or fourth warp end (Diag. 122). Weave a pass in plain weave and beat firmly. It is the plain woven rows between the loops which hold them in place. Don't try to make too many loops too closely together in one row as there is a danger they could slip out.

There are interesting design possibilities with this technique, as with chaining, soumak and twining. Patterns and shapes which are textured in this way look very good in relief against a plain woven ground. Pulled weft motifs can consist of multi-coloured wefts as well as fancy yarns such as bouclé or mohair. If you use very highly spun yarn, the loops will automatically twist (Diag. 122). See p. 18 for re-spinning yarns.

Wrapping

Wrapping is a method of binding various threads around a core to make a strong, pliable rope or cord which can be used in weaving as part of the structure or as decorative detail. Wrapping techniques were used in basket making during the Neolithic Age, when vegetable fibres such as reeds, rushes and straw, were bound together to make baskets, matting, cradles and forms of primitive shelter. Weavers today have found that wrapping offers great structural potential, whether used alone or with other weaving techniques, to create pieces of work which move out of two dimensions into textile sculpture.

The core around which the threads are wrapped is usually larger and thicker than the individual threads. It can be sisal, jute, rope or simply groups of threads. Fringes on the ends of braids can be wrapped by taking the ends in groups, as can the cut warp ends on the top and bottom of tapestries. Wrapping warp ends in a tapestry can create open spaces in the weave, and if additional core threads are attached to the existing warp and wrapped this can be a very effective way of creating tree forms (see colour photo of weaving by Maggie Stewart, after p. 80). To add extra wrapped threads to the weaving, tie the core thread firmly to the warp at the back, wrap tightly, and then secure again at the back.

Diag. 123a and b show you how to begin to wrap, starting at the top and working downwards, trapping the end inside the wrapping. You can darn the other end inside the wrapping when complete either with a needle (Diag. 123c) or pull it through with a crochet hook (Diag. 123d) and finally trim the end (Diag. 123e). Alternatively, you can wrap from bottom to top, and pull the end downwards when complete; this is useful for fringes where the wrapping thread becomes part of the fringe when pulled through and so is invisible. Diags. 123f, g and h show how to change colour by looping one coloured thread through another and trapping the ends inside the wrapping. For thicker wrapping, use two cores, and bind in a figure of eight, (Diag. 123i and j). The core for wrapping should be fairly stiff and the wrapping threads should be bound tightly so they completely cover the core.

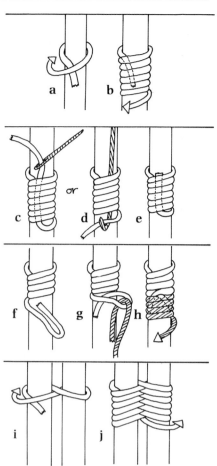

Diagram 123

Wrapping gives exciting possibilities for adding extra layers to an otherwise flat woven surface. Here the background weave and wrapping are in space-dyed yarn so interesting coloured stripes occur. Woven by the author.

Pictorial tapestry

Tapestry is the only form of weaving where realistic pictorial images can be created, and as such it has been unique in textiles as a means of depicting historical events, myths and legends. Because it is possible to create such powerful imagery in tapestry it has become a medium which has attracted many contemporary painters as well as weavers, and woven tapestry is now as much an art form as a craft.

Pictorial tapestry can be representational or abstract. Pictorial subjects in tapestry are, however, handled most successfully when the weaver fully exploits the structural and textural qualities in the weave, and realises that the nature of the craft itself limits what can be done. Early examples of tapestry show how successfully simple shapes, a few colours and hatching were combined to create pictures, and this is particularly apparent in the fragments we have from Ancient Egypt and the wall hangings woven in mediaeval Europe.

The structure of tapestry—that is, the relationship of the weft-faced weave to the direction of the warp—is also a major consideration when planning a pictorial tapestry. The image of the picture does not necessarily have to be upright in relation to the warp; it can be sideways. If there are mainly vertical lines in the picture then turning it sideways to the warp will avoid the problem of too many vertical slits creating weak points in the weaving, and there being rather rigid, stepped outlines to shapes which need to be more fluid. A picture whose movement is mainly horizontal can be woven successfully with the weft running across it.

In this chapter I have discussed these and other points and also introduced new techniques for making curved wefts and colour blending which will add to your weaving vocabulary.

Detail from 'Falconry', one of the *Devonshire Hunting Tapestries*, 1430s. The cartoon was placed sideways to the warp so when the tapestry is hung, the weft is vertical, as shown here. The result is natural movement in the man's face and in the falcons, making them look extremely alive and realistic.

Pictorial tapestry can be a very stimulating and satisfying medium to work in. If you are interested in drawing, painting or photography I am sure you will find your visual ideas can be extended and adapted in the weaving. If you are hesitant about your artistic skills, however, go to exhibitions and look at paintings, try to learn to look and see things around you more, so you absorb ideas which, however simple, you can use in your tapestry weaving.

Curved wefts

So far I have described techniques where the weft is horizontal or at an angle to the warp. It is, however, possible to pass the weft through the warp in such a way that it curves. This opens up far more possibilities for weaving the naturalistic shapes which occur in pictorial subjects. Curved, or eccentric wefts as they are sometimes called, were used a great deal in Coptic and Peruvian tapestries as well as the early mediaeval hangings, for example *The Devonshire Hunting Tapestries* (see colour photo facing p. 81) and by looking at these examples we can see how lively and expressive tapestry can be.

When you have learned to use curved wefts, compare the result with the techniques described on p.72 for weaving circles and curved shapes with stepped horizontal wefts and see the difference. When you plan the design for a tapestry which has curved shapes think which of the techniques can best express your idea.

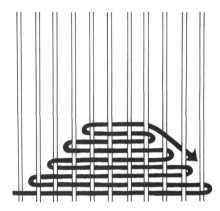

Diagram 124

Curving the weft around horizontally woven shapes

There are two ways to weave shapes with curved wefts. In this, the first method, the weaving is begun with horizontal wefts. Start by passing the weft across a number of warp ends for a few passes, then begin to decrease gradually. This need not be done in a regular sequence like weaving a triangle, but can be built up more freely. If you are following the lines of a cartoon, align the weaving to the shape in the design. Having built up the basic shape, pass the weft around the shape for a few passes so that it takes on a curved edge (Diags. 124 and 125). Bear in mind that the angles of the shape shouldn't be more than 45° or they will be too steep to pass the weft around successfully and it won't beat down well. Take care that the first curved pass is fairly slack so you can beat the weft down around the stepped edges of the shape, or you will have gaps in the weaving.

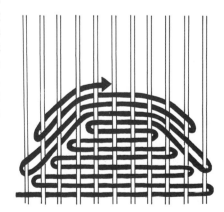

Diagram 125

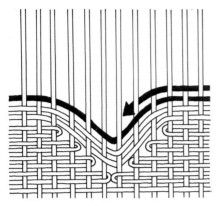

Diagram 126

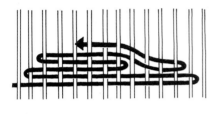

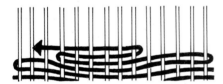

Diagram 127

Outlining

If you want to outline a shape with a contrasting colour using this method, then use the same coloured weft as your basic shape for the first curved pass, to neaten and cover the stepped edges, then change colour in the next pass (Diag. 126).

Having made the weft curve in this way, you will eventually make it straighten out again if you carry on weaving normal passes. The second method of starting curved wefts described below is also useful as a means of making the weft continue to curve.

Weaving extra passes to make curved shapes

Introduce the weft into the warp at the place where you want to begin. Weave a pass over a number of warp ends, then in the next pass turn about two-thirds of the way across, and return over a few warp ends in the opposite shed. Take the weft across the shape again in the opposite shed (Diag. 127). In this way you are weaving an extra pass in the middle of each pass, and if you continue to do this the shape will gradually curve and build up in the centre. Only make one extra pass at a time and turn the weft around on different warp ends each time. The curves you make can be as deep or as shallow as you want, depending on how long you continue to add extra passes. This method can also be used to fill in a dip in the weaving, which is useful to know if your weaving should be horizontal at the top, but isn't! (Diag. 127.)

Shapes made entirely with curved wefts

Shapes which are woven entirely with curved wefts appear very fluid and give a real sense of movement to tapestry. I described how to weave circles with horizontal wefts on p.72 so here I will go through the steps for a circle with curved wefts, and you can try this and compare the two. The background area for the lower half of the circle is woven first in exactly the same way as described on p. 72. This is done with horizontal wefts which are decreased to follow the curved edge of the circle (Diag. 128a). The weft for the circle is then curved into the dip and is woven continuously from one side to the other, slowly decreasing warp ends until you finish on the centre two (Diag. 128a). Build up the top half of the circle, starting from the centre with the same weft and increasing outwards. Finally weave the background area to the left and right of the circle with horizontal wefts again (Diag. 128b and c).

Curved wefts can be used in a very free manner to depict all kinds of soft rounded shapes and work particularly well for natural forms such as leaves, trees and flowers as well as figures, animals and faces. It is important to have guidelines for the shapes you want to weave, whether it is a photograph or sketch beside your weaving, a scaled-up cartoon attached to the back of the warp, or the design inked directly onto the warp ends (see pages 90 to 93).

Once you have the shapes you are weaving clearly in view, you can introduce different coloured wefts so they curve within and follow the outlines of each shape in the picture. Diag. 129 shows how the weft can travel in an eccentric way to build up curved shapes, adding extra passes and extending one shape into another. Make sure each successive weft is in the opposite shed from the previous one and if problems arise when you want to run a continuous weft across two shapes which are in different sheds, make an extra half-pass over one to compensate.

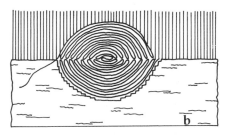

Weaving more detailed shapes on a double warp

A double warp wound on a frame gives more flexibility as to the amount of detail that can be woven in a tapestry. This is because some parts of the weaving can be woven on double warp ends, and when a smaller or more intricate shape is needed you can separate the double warp ends into singles, and pass the weft through individual warp ends, thus giving you twice as many warp ends for particular shapes. This can distort the weaving a little unless you are careful to select a finer weft for those detailed shapes on single warp ends, and it is important to do this.

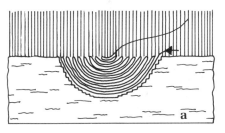

Use a finer cotton warp for double warping and wind twice as many warp ends as usual on the frame (see p. 55). For the heading, twining or turn-back (see p. 56), keep the warp ends in pairs. It is a good idea to make a small sample for this method, so you can try different thicknesses of yarn to find the most suitable for both the double and single warp spacing and to ensure that in both cases the wefts beat down easily and cover the warp.

Diagram 128

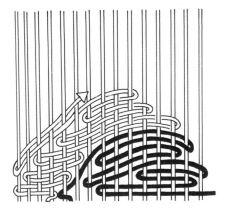

Diagram 129

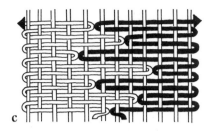

c

b

a

Diagram 130

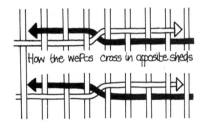

How the wefts cross in opposite sheds

Diagram 131

Mixing colour in the weave

It is possible to give depth and subtlety to colour in tapestry by mixing colour in the weave. In tapestry, just as in painting, the juxtaposition of different colours can alter the feel and the balance of the finished picture. (For more about colour see p. 101). These are some techniques which can be used to mix, brighten, lighten or darken colours.

Hatching

Hatching, or 'meet and separate', was one of the main techniques used in the early mediaeval tapestries for colour shading. By running lines of one colour into another the illusion of a third colour is created, for example, blue running across into yellow and vice versa gives a shade of green in between. The best of the mediaeval tapestries were able to convey very intricate forms and shading with the use of a limited range of dyed yarns. Hatching in tapestry is very like shading in drawing, and can transform a flat picture into something which has form and dimension.

To begin an area of hatching, start the ends of two different coloured wefts in the centre of the shape you are going to weave. Then take the two wefts in opposite directions to the edges of the shape, both in the same shed (Diag. 130a). This is the separating row.

In the next half-pass, the meeting row, the wefts come together again in the opposite shed, but this time meet in a different position from where they began (Diag. 130b). Turn the wefts around on adjacent warp ends and weave to the edges again. The wefts continue to meet and separate in this way, the meeting point always varying on each pass, until an area of shading has been made between the two solid colours on either side (Diag. 130c). To counterchange the outer areas of solid colour, the wefts can be finished off at the edges either side and changed over, or alternatively can be crossed at a meeting point (Diag 131). Any number of wefts can meet and separate simultaneously as long as adjacent wefts either meet with or separate from their neighbour (Diag. 132). If you run out of weft in any one colour or want to change colour, then finish off one end and start a new one in the normal way (see p. 61).

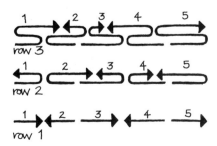

1 2 3 4 5
row 3

1 2 3 4 5
row 2

1 2 3 4 5
row 1

Diagram 132

Opposite: detail from a landscape of mountains and lakes. Here meet and separate and stippling techniques were used to create reflections in the water. Woven by the author.

Stippling

Another method of shading colours in the weave is to use stippling which introduces spots or flecks of one colour onto a background colour.

One or two passes are made in one colour followed by a half-pass in another colour. This results in tiny dots of one colour on a contrasting ground (Diag. 133). The number of passes in the ground colour can vary depending on how dense you want the stippling to be, and you can also change either of the colours around or substitute others if you want to shade subtly from one colour to another. This method can be used very successfully to make a colour lighter or darker—for example, dark blue stippling on a medium blue ground can shade it, that is make it darker. Pale blue stippling on a medium blue ground can tint it, that is make it lighter. The intensity (the brightness or dullness of a colour) can also be affected; for example, stippling a yellow area with purple would make the yellow duller, or stippling a red area with orange or deep pink would make the red more vibrant. The use of hatching and stippling can lift an otherwise rather plain, flat area of the weaving, and give the colours more resonance. For more about colour and weave, see p. 101.

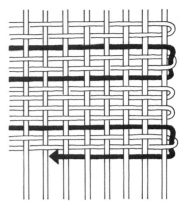

Diagram 133

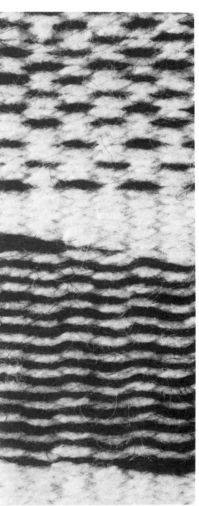

Top: stippling
Bottom: hatching

Blending wefts

Mixing several strands of yarn together and weaving them simultaneously as one weft can produce a much greater depth and softness to colours than weaving areas with a single coloured weft. You can also extend a limited number of coloured yarns into a much wider range.

By stranding four or five yarns together and changing the strands during the weaving, colours can be altered in shade and intensity across the tapestry. It is necessary to use much finer yarns to do this, the ideal yarn being woollen worsted, varying in thickness from 2/12's to 2/18's for a warp spacing of six to eight ends per 2.5 cm (1 in). Try a sample first with varying amounts of yarn stranded together, to assess what the finished thickness of the weft should be for the warp spacing, and ensuring that the weft beats down well and covers the warp.

When you have decided on the correct number of strands you can wind the yarns into butterflies. Let's say, for example, you are going to weave an area of green, using five strands. Rather than use only green yarns, you could mix greens and yellows to lighten and brighten the green area. Take one strand of green and four of yellow and wind them together into a butterfly. Make another butterfly of two green and three yellow strands, three green and two yellow, and so on. Weaving with blended wefts in this way will help you discover a lot about colour and how you can change the darkness, lightness and intensity of a colour. You will find that you can achieve quite marked changes by altering only one strand at a time. A coloured area can have far more depth if different tones of the same colour are blended together, rather than a single weft in one colour, and you can gradate two very contrasting colours from one into the other by gradually changing one strand at a time.

Diagram 134

Interpreting a picture in tapestry

Tapestry weaving is carried out within the restrictions imposed by the vertical warp and the predominantly horizontal weft. Because of these limitations you need to decide whether the picture you have chosen to weave is a suitable subject for tapestry, and if it is, what the best way is to interpret it in the weave. Should the picture be woven upright or sideways?

Let's look at two examples to explain this (Diag. 134). I have exaggerated the pictures a little to make the point. In picture **a** the angle of the mountains and their reflections in the water give a strong sense of direction across the picture. The water, with its rippled surface, could be woven very well with the hatching technique, and the angles of the mountains are not so steep as to present problems with horizontal wefts, so I suggest that this picture would be woven most successfully with the picture upright in relation to the warp.

Picture **b**, however, poses the opposite problem. The curved lines of the woman's face and hair and the curtains at the windows all have a vertical emphasis. If you were to weave this picture upright there would be a great many long slits or interlocked joins in the weaving which could be untidy and weaken the tapestry. By turning the picture sideways though, the fluid lines of the hair and the curtains could be much better woven with curved wefts. Part of the window frame would then become a sharp vertical but as it is only a small part of the picture it could be interlocked in the weave, or stitched afterwards. If you turn the picture sideways you will see how much easier it would be to weave the picture sideways to the warp.

Weaving a tapestry with the image sideways also gives a particularly lively feeling to the subjects in the picture when hung the right way up. Many of the mediaeval tapestries were woven in this way as much of the subject matter had a naturalistic feel to it, with a vertical emphasis.

Making a cartoon

A tapestry can be started without necessarily having a plan, but just a theme in mind. Many weavers, however, find it easier to work from a prepared design. This design is known as the cartoon and is a simple line drawing on white paper, outlining the main shapes to be woven, scaled up to the planned size of the tapestry and taped to the frame behind the warp. This enables you to see the guidelines clearly and to relate the weaving in progress to the initial design.

How rigidly you want to adhere to your original design is your personal choice. I myself think tapestry weaving, as it *is* a craft, should interpret the design within the limitations of the craft, rather than force the weaving to be a copy of an intricately planned design. Also, tapestry is a craft with great creative potential, so letting the feeling for materials, the weave structure and the use of colour come through as the weaving progresses will produce a far more lively and successful result than a rigid weaving by numbers approach. Let's just say that the cartoon contains the basic outlines of the picture to help you keep the shapes and proportions accurate while you are weaving, but it is also a springboard from which you, the weaver, can translate your ideas into the tapestry.

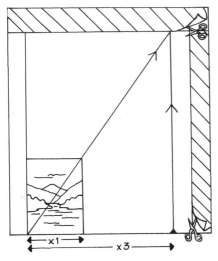

Diagram 135

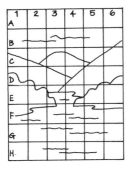

Diagram 136

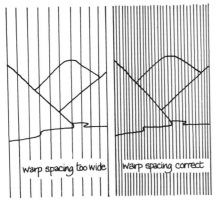

Diagram 137

Scaling up the design

Having decided on your design, you then scale it up to the finished size for your tapestry. To do this, you will need tracing paper, a large sheet of paper the size of your tapestry plus margins, pencil, ruler, black felt-tipped pen and scissors.

Trace the main shapes in the design, omitting too much detail. Trace around the edges too, and cut it out. Draw a margin of at least 7.5 cm (3 in) on the left edge of the sheet of paper, and position the tracing in the bottom left corner, fixing it with paper clips (Diag. 135). Decide how much larger you want the finished weaving to be. If it is to be scaled up three times then multiply the width of the tracing by three, e.g. if the tracing is 20 cm (8 in) wide, the finished width will be 60 cm (24 in). Mark the finished width along the bottom of the paper, then draw a vertical line up from the mark. Draw a diagonal line through the tracing and across the paper until it touches the vertical line. This is the finished depth. Now draw a line across the top and you have the scaled-up size. Add a margin on the right edge and trim off the rest of the paper (Diag. 135).

Unclip the tracing, draw a grid on it and number and letter the squares (Diag. 136). Do the same on the paper, making the squares proportionately larger, e.g. 2.5 cm (1 in) squares on the tracing will be 7.5 cm (3 in) squares on the paper if you have scaled up the design three times the size.

Copy the lines within each square on the tracing onto the paper. At this stage you may want to adjust, add or remove some lines. Look at larger areas and see if they make satisfactory shapes. Remember that background areas are positive shapes as much as figures or objects in the foreground. Also bear in mind that the weaving will add texture to areas in the design and the way you use colour will give light, shade and form, so don't over-complicate the design on the cartoon.

Before you finalise the shapes in the cartoon and warp up the frame you will need to think carefully about the warp spacing. The closer the warp spacing, the greater the detail you can get into your weaving. Think first whether your design is to be woven upright or sideways to the warp (see p. 90) and then look at the shapes in the design and estimate a practical warp spacing (Diag. 137). I would suggest a warp spacing of four, six or eight ends per 2.5 cm (1 in) is generally suitable. When you are satisfied with your design go over the lines with a black felt-tip pen.

Placing the cartoon behind the warp

Warp up your frame according to the spacing you have decided on. The cartoon is taped to the sides of the frame behind the warp (Diag. 138). The bottom edge of the cartoon should line up with the twining, or the top of the turn-back. When you are weaving always look through the warp to the cartoon at eye level, or your design will become distorted. This means you have to alter your working position in relation to the frame, or move the frame itself, as the weaving progresses.

Inking the design onto the warp

This is an alternative to having a paper cartoon behind the warp. You still need to make a cartoon first, as already described, before you can trace the design onto the warp. It can be an advantage if, because of the type of weaving frame, the paper cartoon would be too close to the warp and impede your progress, or alternatively a little too far back from the warp, so it would be difficult to read the lines accurately.

Position the cartoon immediately behind the warp, and pin it in place with long pins, such as hat pins. Use a permanent black felt pen or Indian ink to trace the lines in the cartoon onto the warp. A non-permanent pen will discolour the weft. Rotate each warp end as you mark it (Diag. 139) so the warp is inked all round. The warp does twist slightly during weaving and if you only mark the front of the warp, you could find your marks have slowly disappeared as you progress up the warp. When all the design is inked onto the warp, remove the cartoon but keep it by you as a guide.

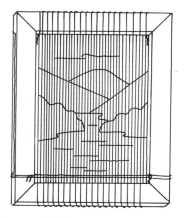

Diagram 138

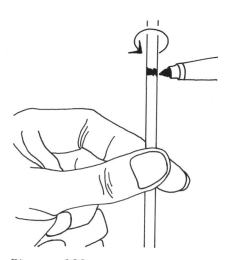

Diagram 139

Finishing tapestries

The finish and presentation of your tapestry is vital both from the visual point of view and the practical one if it is to last in good condition. Finishing a tapestry should do justice to the work you put into it, so take time and care and it will be worthwhile .

Removing the tapestry from the frame

First complete the weaving at the top with a finished edging in the same way as you started. This can either be twining, half-hitch knots, or a turn-back (see p. 56). Start to cut the warp at the top and bottom, working from the centre outwards to the corners, so the weaving is suspended in the frame until the corner warp ends are cut. Keep the ends as long as you can by cutting them right on the edges of the frame or on the nails and secure them with overhand knots or darn the ends to the back (Diag. 140). Darn in any ends from the twining or other edging and pull the heading out altogether.

Darning in wefts
For smaller tapestries which you aren't going to back, darn in all the wefts vertically at the back with a blunt, large-eyed needle, for about 5 cm (2 in), and trim.

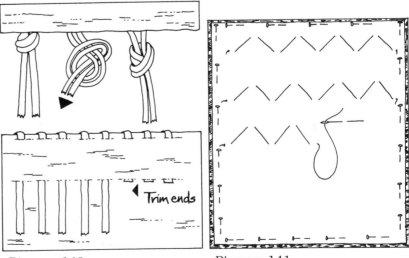

Trim ends

Diagram 140   Diagram 141

Backing a tapestry

The backing will protect your tapestry from dust and will therefore lengthen its life. Backing is especially advisable for larger tapestries. Pre-shrunk cotton calico or curtain lining are cheap, suitable fabrics to use. You do not need to darn in all the ends at the back in this case, except for any wefts which could work their way out to the front, e.g. at a weak colour junction, or where you have finished slits in the weave.

Cut the backing fabric so it is 5 cm (2 in) larger all round than the tapestry. Lay your tapestry face down on the table and place the backing over it. Fold all the edges under and pin the backing to the tapestry, making sure the backing is quite loose and isn't pulling in from the edges. Use a cotton thread and sew across the width in rows about 15 cm (6 in) apart using a diagonal stitch (Diag. 141). Take care to catch the sewing thread only lightly into the warp of the tapestry, so it doesn't show on the front. Hem stitch the folded edges all around the backing. Cut another strip of fabric slightly narrower than the backing and 15 cm (6 in) deep. Fold under a 1.75 cm ($\frac{1}{2}$ in) hem and stitch this to the backing at the top, leaving both ends open. A pole, either wooden, brass or steel can then be inserted on which to hang the tapestry (Diag. 142).

Some tapestries may need weighting slightly at the lower edge for them to hang better. Tiny lead weights encased in cotton, (used for curtains) can be bought in haberdashers by the metre or yard and these can be stitched into the hem at the lower edge of the backing.

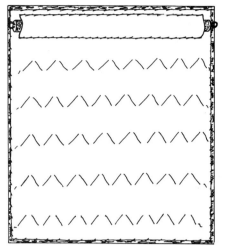

Diagram 142

Hanging a tapestry

There are many ways to hang a tapestry apart from the one described above. You can attach velcro to the backing and to a wooden baton on the wall, or tiny eye-hooks into a flat baton inserted into the backing which hook onto cup-hooks on the wall. Here are two simple suggestions for small unbacked tapestries.

The simplest way of all is to hang the weaving from a wooden stick. It can be round or flat, painted a matching or contrasting colour or stained with wood-dye. Alternatively, use metal or perspex rods if they would complement the weaving. Insert the stick into the warp at the top while it is still on the frame. As you cut the warp ends tie them in pairs around the stick (Diag. 143).

Another method: cut the warp from the frame but do not tie the warp ends in knots. Cut four pieces of wood, the same width as your weaving. Trim your fringes to the same depth as the wood and glue two pieces of wood together, trapping the fringes firmly between the wood, at both the top and bottom of the weaving. Use very strong glue and weight the wood down until thoroughly dry (Diag. 143). Whichever way you hang a tapestry, remember it should relate to the design and enhance the weaving, not overpower it.

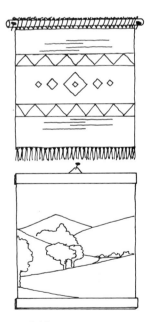

Diagram 143

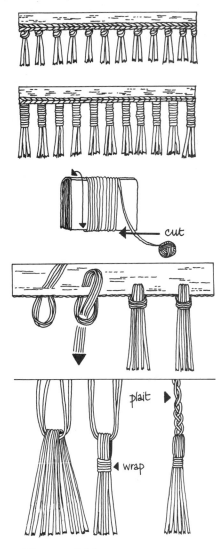

Diagram 144

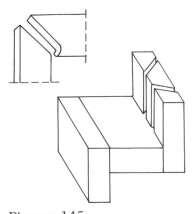

Diagram 145

Fringes and decorative edges

The simplest edging for tapestries and rugs is an edging in twining (see p. 56) and a knotted fringe, using the cut warp ends as fringes. Tie the warp ends in pairs in overhand knots (Diag. 140).

A more colourful edge is to wrap the cut warp ends with wool, although your ends will need to be a reasonable length to make this effective. See p. 83 for wrapping.

If you want a thicker, more elaborate fringe, you can darn in the cut warp ends to the back of the weaving (Diag. 140) and add fringes or tassels made from other threads as shown in Diag. 144. You can design and weave decorative edges to your tapestries, particularly if you don't want the weaving to have straight edges. These edges should relate to and be an integral part of the whole design, though, rather than just being added in an arbitrary way. I have included some ideas on p. 97 and the colour photo facing p. 96 also shows a variety of edges on finished pieces of weaving.

Mounting or framing a tapestry

Tapestry produces a textile which is soft and tactile, so hanging it simply often enhances its qualities the most. However very small pieces can look rather lost when removed from the frame and hung up, so it can sometimes be more suitable to mount or frame them (see p. 97). First finish the tapestry by darning in all the warp ends at the back. If the weaving isn't quite square then block it out on the ironing board with pins, and lightly steam press it into shape.

To mount a tapestry you will need two pieces of 1.75 cm ($\frac{1}{2}$ in) thick softboard or blockboard. One piece should be the same size as your tapestry, the other approximately 7.5 cm (3 in) larger all round. You will also need some plain woven or other suitable fabric which you feel complements the tapestry. Spread fabric glue across the larger board and stretch a piece of the fabric smoothly across the board and over the edges, neatly mitring the corners. Do the same with the smaller board, then glue it firmly to the centre of the larger board with strong glue. Place your tapestry on the smaller board and catch it down with sewing thread, making invisible stitches around the edges. The tapestry itself will stand out on the mounted board and the border around it will set it off well (see photo on p. 97).

To frame a tapestry you can buy a simple, suitable frame (without glass), but I will describe here a method of making your own. You will need wooden beading with a narrow overlapping edge for the frame, and some 1.75 cm ($\frac{1}{2}$ in) thick softboard or chipboard the same size as your weaving. Cut the board to the size of your tapestry. Drill two small holes near the top and insert thin wire through them to hang the frame by. Spread fabric glue on the board and stretch a piece of cotton or woven fabric across it. Place the tapestry on top and catch it down with sewing

Finishing needs as much consideration as planning and carrying out the weaving. Shown here are shaped edges (top) and wrapped edges (centre and left) for tapestry and fringed, plaited and corded edges on braids.

Ideas for tapestry can often be found in drawings or photographs of natural forms. This is a miniature tapestry of an iris; the flower was woven sideways to the warp, using fine silks on a wool ground. Woven by Eileen Martin.

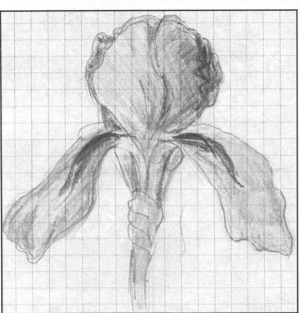

thread, making invisible stitches around the edges. Paint or stain the beading and let it dry.

Cut the beading for the four sides of the board, making mitred corners at each end of all the pieces. You can make or buy a simple block for cutting these (Diag. 145). Glue the beading to the edge of the board with strong wood glue, overlapping the edges over the tapestry. If your weaving is thick or textured you can cut the board slightly larger than the weaving so the beading butts up to the edges. Secure the beading with elastic bands until it is thoroughly dry.

Another alternative is to leave the weaving on the frame permanently. Make a simple frame and paint or stain it before you warp it up. For miniature weaving, make a frame with wooden dowel and glue the pieces together.

Put triangular templates at the bottom of the warp to make a shaped edge

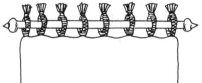

Wrap groups of warp ends at the top and loop them over a pole

Make slits in the weaving at the top and loop it over a pole

Diagram 146

Miniature tapestries often look lost when removed from the frame, so careful thought is needed about finishing and mounting. Left to right: weaving mounted on linen covered board; face in its frame; weaving mounted and edged with wooden beading. Woven by the author.

Designing for weaving

Detail from a weaving, showing a scene through an arch. The cartoon is placed behind the warp, so the shapes to be woven can be seen clearly. Woven by the author.

What is design?

Design is one of those words we all get confused by; what exactly does it mean? Essentially, designing is about planning something purposefully, and, with weaving or any craft, this will mean making choices which are appropriate for the medium you are working in. And it is important, too, to think about how your idea can be interpreted through the particular weaving techniques you will be using.

For example, a potter, when planning a pot, will make choices about the type of clay to use, the form the pot will take, its size, its function, if there will be surface patterns decorating the pot, and if glazes will be used for colour, surface texture and finish. When the viewer looks at the pot, he or she sees the finished product, the outcome of these choices, perhaps not being fully aware of how much decision-making took place as the potter was moulding the clay into shape.

In any piece of work there is, however, more than just the craftsmanship that was involved in the making process. There is another, more abstract element involved and that is its aesthetic content. The pot, if it has succeeded, is not only suitable for its purpose, the right size and made in the most practical way. It is also pleasing to the eye. The aesthetic quality of a piece of work is its most unique and indefinable feature, and is the fruition of the designer's ideas. This is why it is impossible to say definitively whether a design is good or bad and why there isn't a set formula we can learn to produce unfailingly good designs.

If there aren't any set rules on design, there are, however, certain precepts which I think apply when designing, and you can use these as guidelines when you are planning and working on a piece of weaving. I have outlined these in this chapter, in the hope that they might help you and heighten your visual awareness. Most of all, don't be intimidated by the word 'design'. There are ideas all around you, so keep your eyes open and you will soon begin to absorb all sorts of images you can use in your weaving. Try to devote a table and some wall-space to your weaving ideas and make a collection of things that interest you, such as natural objects, yarns, fibres and fabrics chosen for colour and texture, sketches, photographs, either your own or cut from magazines, postcards from museums, absolutely anything that you find is visually stimulating. With these things around you, and your weaving samples and current projects in view, your approach to designing will be a natural and relaxed one.

Designing for weaving

The foremost consideration in designing for weaving is to have a clear understanding of the techniques involved, so you can be sensitive to the limitations of the craft. This is why constantly trying out small samples worked in the weaving techniques described in the main part of the book is an invaluable way of finding out what does or doesn't work well. This applies whether you are a beginner or already have some expertise. These experimental samples, whether for braids or tapestry, will help you to learn a lot about the interaction of yarns, colour, texture and pattern, and develop a good understanding of the different weave structures. They can also be a constant reference for ideas for larger projects.

When you start to plan a piece of weaving, you are beginning the design process, and the practical knowledge you have already gained will help you to make the necessary choices about your proposed project. First of all then, let's try to see what is involved in designing for weaving. To simplify the design process, I will break it down into two kinds of choice; the practical, and the aesthetic.

Practical elements of design consist of:

1 Shape and size
2 Weave structure
3 Choice of yarns for colour and texture
4 Choice of shapes for pattern or pictorial imagery
5 Craftsmanship and choice of techniques
6 Whether the work is functional or decorative

Aesthetic elements in design consist of:

1 Source of ideas
2 Choice of yarns to interpret the idea in the weave successfully
3 Choice and use of colour, texture, pattern or shape in the weaving to interpret the idea successfully
4 Balance and proportion
5 Contrast

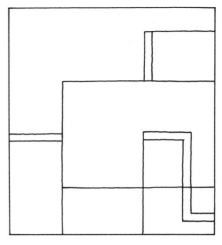

Diagram 147

Diagram 148

Shape

The shape made by the perimeter of your weaving as well as the shapes used within the design, whether for pattern or pictorial images, will be influenced by your choice of weave structure, in this case braid or tapestry weave. In tapestry you could decide to work within a rectangle and to echo this by dividing the area into square and rectangular shapes to make a simple abstract design (Diag. 147). Alternatively, you could make a design using only curves, ovals and flowing lines to express movement (Diag. 148). In both these examples, limited use of a very simple shape has been made and this can often be the basis for a strong yet uncluttered design.

Diagram 149

Diagram 150

In braid weaving the shape of the finished piece will be long and narrow, so it is very suitable for practical items such as belts, sashes and straps. You can of course join several braids together, to make larger pieces of weaving, for rugs, bags etc, or for decorative purposes like wall-hangings, screens or panels. Consider how the narrow braids can be joined in different ways (see p. 108) remembering that the finished piece should make a pleasing combination of the different colours and patterns woven in the braids.

In simple terms, shapes are either geometric, so that they can be drawn mathematically, the basic shapes being a square, circle and triangle, or organic, that is made up of fluid lines giving a feeling of growth and movement (Diag. 149). They can also be a combination of these two. All shapes have positive and negative aspects; the positive shape is that within the edges, which most of us see, and the negative shapes are those which meet the outside edges of the shape, and are equally important to consider when designing. Try looking closely at things around you and train your eye to see both these kind of shapes (Diag. 150).

Balance and proportion

The wrong balance in a design can make it seem top-heavy or lop-sided. The easiest way of keeping true balance is to make a design which is perfectly symmetrical, but shapes which make an assymmetrical design can still be balanced if the design as a whole is evenly weighted, (Diag. 151). Look at the distribution of shapes in a design, their proportions in relation to one another. Ask yourself if your eye settles easily on a focal point which the other shapes complement or if it gets distracted by different shapes competing with one another, making the whole design disturbing to look at.

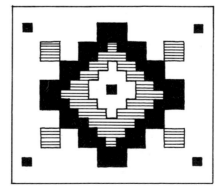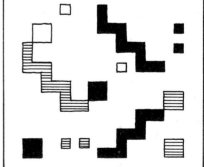

Diagram 151

Colour

Of all the elements in designing for weaving, colour is probably the most elusive to work with. Colour is charged with emotional and psychological meaning and so is the most personal means of expression. Colours are never seen in isolation but always in relation to one another, and are influenced by quantity, shape and light in how we perceive them.

In weaving, no less than in any other art or craft form, colour is vital and if we are to learn how to control it we need to understand what its qualities are and how we react to it. I couldn't begin to explain colour in scientific terms and I think it can be inhibiting to theorise about it too much because ultimately choice and use of colour is based on your own feelings and perceptions. All I can attempt to do here is to outline the properties of colour and how they react to one another and hope that this, combined with your own likes and dislikes, will help you to increase your colour awareness so you can try some new and exciting colour combinations in your weaving. Some definitions of colour vocabulary follow, which I hope will be useful to you.

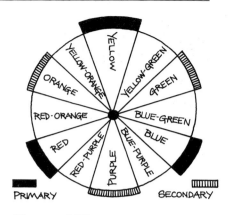

Diagram 152

Primary colours
There are three primary colours, red, yellow and blue. These cannot be obtained from other colours, but when mixed make all other colours (Diag. 152).

Secondary colours
Mixing the three primaries gives the secondary colours, that is red + yellow = green, red + blue = purple, and blue + yellow = green. (Diag. 152.)

Tertiary colours
The tertiary colours are those colours which are between the primaries and the secondaries on the colour wheel, e.g. yellow-orange, red-purple etc. (Diag. 152). Try making a colour wheel, using yarns wrapped around a circle of stiff card (see colour photo facing p. 104), so you can see how the colours relate to one another.

Any colour or hue, that we see on the colour wheel or in a rainbow is in its purest state. Apart from its hue, colour also has value and intensity. Value is the lightness or darkness of a colour in relation to black and white. All the colours on the wheel are not of the same value; yellow is the lightest, purple the darkest. One colour can have a scale of values, e.g. from the palest to the deepest blue. Intensity, or saturation, describes the brightness or dullness of a colour. A pure colour is the most intense. It can be made less so by mixing it with grey, black, white or the colour opposite it on the wheel, so red on the circle is very intense, but mixed with green it will appear duller.

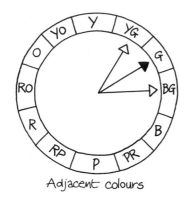

Adjacent colours

Diagram 153

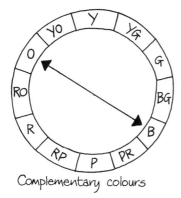

Complementary colours

Diagram 154

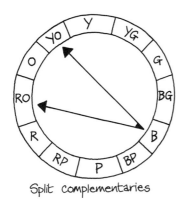

Split complementaries

Diagram 155

Colour can also appear warm or cool. If you have painted the walls of a room and looked at the result, you will have realised that blues or greens give a cool feeling whereas pinks or reds create a warmer atmosphere. On the colour wheel it seems that the reds, oranges and yellows are warm, whereas the blues, greens and purples appear cooler. Try wrapping yarns in warm and cool colours around a strip of card to see the effect (photo facing p. 104). Tertiary colours can be on the border of both warm and cool—yellow-green, or red-purple seem to have both qualities. A purple, if it is reddish, appears warm, whereas blue-purple can be cool.

Once we have identified the colours and their properties, we can begin to discover how they react. Look at the colour circle (photo facing p. 104) and try to see how the colours relate. Probably the first thing you will notice is that the colours which are next to one another are harmonious.

Harmony of adjacents
Adjacent or analogous colours blend together, giving a soft, soothing effect. They are the colours often found in nature—autumnal colours ranging from yellows, golds and oranges through to reds and purples, and the yellows, yellow-greens and blue-greens which are reminiscent of early spring.

Using a primary or secondary colour in a harmonious colour scheme is often successful. e.g. green with yellow-green and blue-green (Diag. 153). The primary or secondary colour is enhanced by the adjacents and they in turn reflect its purity.

Harmony of opposites
Harmony is also found in the colours which are directly opposite to one another on the colour circle, and these are called complementary colours (Diag. 154). If you use blue and orange next to each other, each colour heightens the intensity of the other, so much so that they vibrate at the edges. The main complementaries pair a primary with a secondary colour, e.g. blue and orange, red and green, yellow and purple and these give a bold, powerful effect. More subtlety is achieved with the intermediate complementaries, e.g. red-orange, and blue-green, yellow-orange and blue-purple and yellow-green and red-purple. The harmony of split-complementaries is achieved by combining a colour with two others which are adjacent to its opposite (Diag. 155).

Understanding the qualities of colours as described here and developing your own awareness of how colours can be used comes through constant observation, and trying out samples. Look at the examples of weaving whenever you can to see if you think the colours work well together. Some of the illustrations throughout the book may enable you to assess how the colours interact in the finished pieces. The sunset tapestry (facing p. 105) uses soft pale colours which gives a sense of distance; the vibrant red of the sun stands out, but is balanced in the whole composition by the mauve clouds running across it, creating the feeling of a misty evening sky.

The tree (between pp. 80–81) woven in strong dark colours looks dramatic against the subtle blues and pinks of the sky, and shows the use of contrast in colour as well as texture to very good effect. The vibrant use of reds, pinks and blues in the photo facing p. 64 enhances the bold geometric patterns, giving an overall warm, rich quality.

Materials

Your selection of materials will be determined by what you want to weave, its visual effect and its function when completed. A warp must be strong and smooth or it will break. The weft you choose depends on the weave structure and whether you want a matt or shiny look, a soft, textured look using singles, handspun wool, or bouclé, or a firm weave using worsted or rug yarns. Read more about yarns on p. 10. Experiment with different yarns to find out what you like. Setting up a narrow warp and weaving with a variety of yarns in a sampler will help you to understand the nature of materials and how they interact (see photo, p. 106).

Craftsmanship

Skilled craftsmanship is something we admire when we see it in a finished piece of work. Always try to do your very best. As you weave more your skill will improve and you can take on more ambitious projects. Weaving a piece which is very complex, requiring knowledge of techniques you don't have, will result in frustration. Start with something fairly (but not too) simple, weave it very well and you will be spurred on to tackle a more ambitious piece with confidence. Always be prepared to go back and undo or change some part of the weaving which is faulty or unsatisfactory.

Ideas

Ideas are all round us: we can be constantly finding sources of inspiration if we know how to look and see. I described on p. 98 how you can make a collection of things which interest you, and I think this can be invaluable. Just collect what pleases you visually, not consciously connecting this with weaving. Seeing something which is visually interesting and then translating it into an idea for weaving may not be a single step, but it will eventually be worthwhile if you can train yourself to be observant, and then to be selective about what you are going to use for your weaving.

The way shadows fall across the ground on a sunny day, the textures and colours in a wall, catching sight of part of a scene through a gate or a fence; all of these things can trigger off an idea, which may be about shapes, colours, contrast, texture or a pictorial composition. Natural objects, buildings, trees and landscapes, urban or industrial scenes, figures, everyday objects you use are all a source of ideas, and we each perceive them in our own individual way. You may choose to look at an object through a magnifying glass and discover all sorts of detail which might inspire you, or you may prefer to use a camera to enclose within the lens some part of a building which you think makes an interesting composition of abstract shapes.

If you are interested in drawing and painting this will stimulate ideas for weaving. If you feel your artistic skills are limited, however, then keep a notebook of things that interest you; colour combinations you see and like, patterns in rugs and any textiles you would like to weave, photographs you take or find in magazines which could be the basis for an idea. Here are some simple suggestions for an ideas collection:

1 Collect a variety of different types and textures of yarns and threads in cut lengths of about 7.5 cm (3 in). Sort them into colour ranges, e.g. blues, red, pinks, greens etc. and keep them in small boxes or glue onto strips of card and pin to the wall.
2 Keep a box full of small natural objects such as stones, shells, dried leaves, flower-heads, bark. These are interesting sources of pattern and colour when looked at closely.
3 Collect postcards from museums on textiles, historical or contemporary.
4 Ask anyone you know who is going abroad to send any postcards they see of weavers and weaving.
5 Keep photographs of anything which interests you, as well as photos which in themselves are composed of interesting shapes or colours.
6 Jot down patterns or colour combinations you see and like, whether in fabrics, things you see in museums, or out on a walk.

Designing before you weave or as you weave?

This is a choice which depends on how you personally like to work. Weaving spontaneously, with a theme in mind, can be exciting and satisfying. You may be inspired at the start by the colour and texture of your yarns and an idea will grow from this. You may be interested in particular shapes and how they relate to one another. Starting at the beginning and just working through the weaving, keeping to your theme, but allowing arbitrary things like changing shapes, different yarns, even running out of a particular yarn, influence you as you weave, can be a stimulating way to work. In this way you often stumble on ideas which might otherwise not occur to you. Stop and look at the

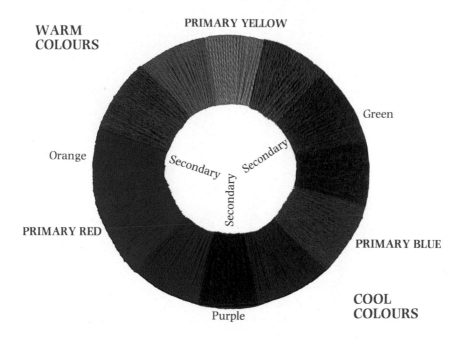

WARM
COLOURS

PRIMARY YELLOW

Green

Orange

Secondary Secondary

Secondary

PRIMARY RED

PRIMARY BLUE

Purple

COOL
COLOURS

Cool/Warm Colours

Cool colour at the centre of
warm colours

Cool colour across warm
colours

Alternating a cool colour with
a warm colour

Colour Harmony

Orange with red-
orange and yellow
orange

Blue with blue-
purple and blue-
green

Yellow-green
with red-violet

Orange with blue

Adjacents: colours adjacent on the
colour circle are complementary

Opposites: colours opposite one another
on the colour circle contrast, but are still
complementary

Ideas from natural forms and landscapes – photographs from the author's collection.

Using knots and loops against flat woven tapestry gives the weaving an exciting tactile surface and a three-dimensional quality. The choice of colour also gives this weaving a strong sense of depth. Woven by Adrienne Tufnail.

weaving often. Weaving in this organic way means you need to respond to what you have done and make decisions about the next step.

There are times, though, when working out a plan is preferable. Tablet weaving is more successful on the whole when a pattern chart has been worked out first (p. 38). In backstrap weaving planning the arrangement of the warp threads is the first step (p.30). In tapestry you can prepare a cartoon before you begin to weave (p. 91). This is especially helpful when weaving curved shapes and when you want to be certain to maintain the balance and proportions of the original design. However, even with a cartoon, be prepared to make changes and be sensitive to how the weaving can best interpret the original idea.

Tapestry by one of the pupils of the Ramses Wissa Wassef School, set up in the early 1950s at Harrania, Egypt. The tapestries are woven spontaneously, without any picture or design. Photo: Werner Forman Archive.

Colour plate:
This tapestry was woven from a watercolour of a sunset. The soft use of colour and the gently curved wefts translate the delicacy of the painting into the weave very well, so that the finished tapestry is both sensitive and yet has a bold image. Woven by Eileen Martin.

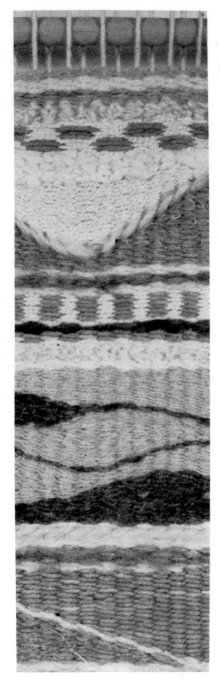

Design exercises

Weaving samples

1 Use a small frame without nails. Wind three narrow warps with different thicknesses of cotton and warp spacing, e.g. four, six and eight ends per 2.5 cm (1 in). Experiment with different yarns and weave structures to see what effects you get. One strip could be tapestry weave, one warp-faced and one using texture techniques. Ideas for braids and tapestry, colour arrangement, contrasting textures etc. can come from samplers like this.

2 Use a small frame and warp it up to four or six ends per 2.5 cm (1 in). Select two contrasting colours, or black and white, and try to weave a balanced design using only stripes, or blocks or triangles.

3 Choose a photograph of a favourite painting. Match yarns to the colours in the painting and wind them around a strip of card. Using this colour scheme, weave a small tapestry sampler to see how the colours blend or contrast with one another. Use hatching, stippling and colour blending (p. 88).

4 Look at a detail of a flower, stone or shell using a magnifying glass. Look at the shapes and colours carefully. Weave a small tapestry sampler which catches the feel of the object. It does not have to be representational.

5 Wind a short cotton warp in two colours and thread tablets as in method 2 (p. 40). Try some of the turning sequences as described in the tablet weaving chapter, but also experiment with changing the positions of the tablets and see what possibilities there are. Try using a very thick weft, to give a 'repp' effect. Separate the tablets into two groups so you weave separate braids, then twist or plait them together.

6 Use different types of strong cotton threads, some matt, some shiny, and in different thicknesses. Wind them around a strip of card until you have a colour and texture combination you like. Use this as a warp for a backstrap braid, selecting either the striped or brocaded technique (p. 35), to emphasise the contrast in texture and colour.

The tapestry sampler can allow you to try out different effects. Top to bottom: vertical bars; soumak around a curved shape; curved wefts; angled shapes. Woven by the author.

Working with cut paper

1 Use different coloured papers and cut into narrow strips of equal width. Arrange them so the colours range from dark to light, warm to cool, or dull to intense, and stick them down onto a sheet of paper. These ideas can be the basis for vertically striped tablet or backstrap woven braids, making each colour an equal number of warp ends. For finger weaving, arrange equal numbers of threads on the pencil and weave as diagonal braid (p. 20).

2 Use different coloured papers and cut into strips in the following proportions: $0+1=1$, $1+1=2$, $1+2=3$, $2+3=5$, $3+5=8$ etc. Fibonacci, a thirteenth-century mathematician, devised this series and the system is that each number is the sum of the previous two. The result is a striped pattern of well-balanced proportions. It can be used for vertically striped braids in which the numbers can represent a measurement or a number of warp ends, and for horizontal stripes in a tapestry woven rug.

3 Use white paper and coloured pencils or pens. Cut the paper into strips of even width. Fill in coloured bands across each strip, varying the width and spacing on each strip. Play around with the strips until you like the arrangement, then stick them down onto a sheet of paper. For backstrap braids, the coloured bands could be worked in brocading on separate braids and then the braids sewn together. For tapestry, this could be an abstract design; the white ground could be woven solidly or there could be slits in the weave as part of the design (see photo).

4 Use old magazines and choose a colour theme, e.g. red and blue. Cut out parts of colour photographs which are shades of red and blue and arrange them in a collage. You could also keep to a theme of shapes as well as colour, such as squares, ovals etc. This is for tapestry ideas. If the shapes are too intricate, be selective and simplify the design.

5 Again, for tapestry ideas, cut a rectangular window in a piece of white paper, about 5×7.5 cm (2×3 in). Run it across photographs, looking for areas which are interesting either because of shape, colour, contrast or texture. Clip the window in place, and trace the area within it. Enlarge the tracing (p. 92), adapting shapes from the original if it improves the overall design.

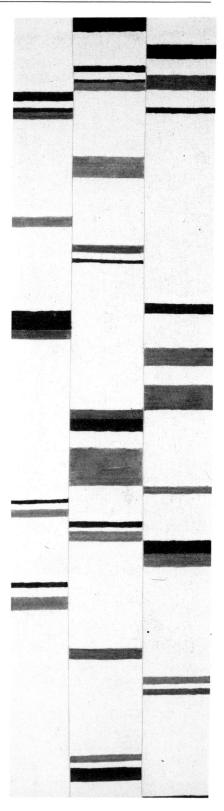

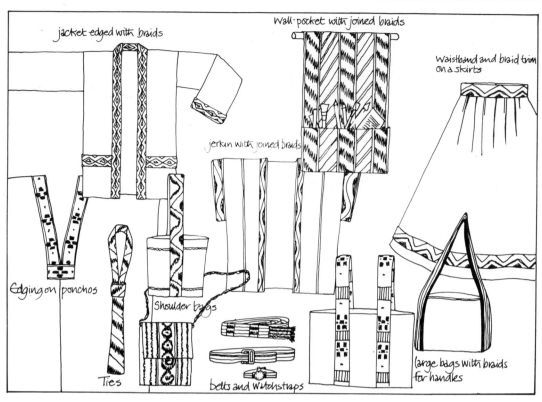

jacket edged with braids

Wall-pocket with joined braids

Waistband and braid trim on a skirts

jerkin with joined braids

Edging on ponchos

Shoulder bags

Ties

belts and watchstraps

large bags with braids for handles

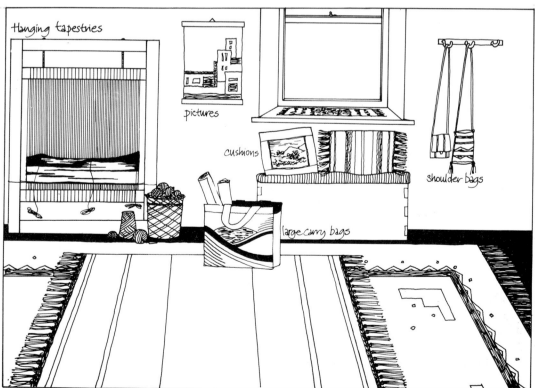

Hanging tapestries

pictures

cushions

shoulder bags

large carry bags

GLOSSARY

Balanced weave   the warp and weft are interwoven so both show equally in the weave; used in some finger weaving

Beater   a tooth-edged comb with a handle, or a fork, used to beat the weft down in tapestry; also a flat, smooth stick used in braid weaving to beat the weft towards the weaver

Brocading   a method of making patterns in backstrap weaving with additional wefts

Butterfly   a small bundle of yarn wound in a figure of eight for tapestry weft

Half-hitch knots   a row of knots tied at the beginning and end of a tapestry to make secure edges

Half-pass   one row of weaving in tapestry

Heading   two cotton threads passed through alternate sheds at the bottom of the warp on a frame

Heddles   cotton loops attached to alternate warp ends

Heddle stick   the stick which holds the heddles, which when pulled opens one shed

Knots   cut lengths of yarn attached to the warp to make a pile weave; the Ghiordes and Sehna knots are two traditional knots still in use

Leashes   cotton loops attached to alternate warp ends, either tied in groups or to a leash bar

Loops   lengths of yarn either wound around or pulled out from the warp to make a looped surface texture

Pass   two rows of weaving in tapestry

Repp   weft threads passed through the warp in groups to make a thicker ribbed weave; used in finger weaving and can be used in tablet weaving

Shed   the V-shaped opening in the warp formed by raising alternate warp ends, through which the weft is passed

Shed stick   flat stick to hold the shed open while weaving

Soumak   lengths of yarn passed in a sequence around the warp to give a patterned surface texture

Twining   carried out at the beginning and end of the weaving to space the warp and make a secure edge; also a decorative weaving technique

Turn-back   a narrow band of plain weaving in cotton woven at the beginning and end of a tapestry for a neat turned-back hem

Warp   the lengthways threads through which the crossways or weft threads are passed

Warp ends   individual warp threads

Warp-faced weave   the warp ends are pulled closely together and held by the weft so only the warp shows on the surface; used for backstrap, tablet and some finger weaving

Weft   the yarn that is interwoven through the warp crossways to form the weaving

Weft-faced weave   the weft is beaten down firmly on a highly tensioned warp so only the weft shows on the surface; tapestry is always in this weave.

BIBLIOGRAPHY

Band weaving   Harold & Sylvia Tacker, Studio Vista (1975)
Making plaits and braids   June Barker, Batsford (1973)
Card weaving   Candace Crockett, Watson-Guptill (1973)
Tablet weaving   Ann Sutton & Pat Holtom, Batsford (1975)
Techniques of tablet weaving   Peter Collingwood, Faber (1982)
Backstrap weaving   Barbara Taber & Marilyn Anderson, Watson-Guptill (1975)
Techniques of Guatemalan weaving   Lena Bjerregaard, Van Nostrand Reinhold (1977)
Textiles of Ancient Peru and their techniques   Raoul D'Harcourt, Univ. of Washington Press (3rd edn. 1977)
Finger weaving: Indian braiding   Alta Turner, Sterling Publishing Co. & Oak Tree Press (4th edn. 1978)
Small woven tapestries   Mary Rhodes, Batsford (1973)
The techniques of woven tapestry   Tadek Beutlich, Batsford (1967)
Frame-loom weaving   Jane Redman, Van Nostrand Reinhold (1976)
The craft of the weaver   Ann Sutton, Peter Collingwood & Geraldine St Aubyn Hubbard, BBC Publications (1982)
The weaving, spinning and dyeing book   Rachel Brown, Routledge & Kegan Paul (1979)
Beyond weaving   Marcia Chamberlain & Candace Crockett, Watson-Guptill (1974)
The techniques of rug weaving   Peter Collingwood, Faber (1968)
The craft of weaving   Irene Waller, Stanley Paul (1976)
The book of looms   Eric Broudy, Studio Vista (1979)
Fine-art weaving   Irene Waller, Batsford (1979)
Drawing on the right side of the brain   Betty Edwards, Fontana/Collins (1982)
The elements of colour   Johannes Itten, Van Nostrand Reinhold (1970)
Design and form   Johannes Itten, Thames & Hudson (revised edn. 1983)
Natural dyes for spinners and weavers   Hetty Wickens, Batsford (1983)

INDEX